Selling In  The Clouds

Ray Collis and John O Gorman

www.sellingintheclouds.com

ISBN: 978-1-907725-01-2

© Ray Collis & John O Gorman

Published by:

The ASG Group
Accelerating Sales Growth
Unit 24 Parkwest Enterprise Centre,
Lavery Avenue, Dublin 12, Ireland.
www.theASGgroup.com

Contents

Acknowledgements

From Ray:

To my family, Jeanette, Kevin and Andreas, this book is for you with love. To my mother Theresa and departed father Desmond, as well as my brothers Damien and Gavin, special thanks for your encouragement and support.

A big thanks also to all those who gave of their advice and participated in our research and workshop programs around this book.

From John:

To my wife Janel and daughter Symone, you both keep me grounded and ensure I stay honest with myself. You are my greatest supporters, despite the sacrifices you both make as I travel around the world.

To my parents, I owe my belief in people, learning and being curious about human behavior to you both. Your unending support and words of encouragement continue to inspire my work and research. This book is more proof that I continue to listen to you both.

Introduction

The Forecast for IT Sales

Cloudy with a chance of rain. That is the forecast for all those selling (and indeed buying) IT solutions 'in the age of the cloud'.

Of course the rain is a metaphor for sales revenue and commissions and the mixed forecast is caused by changes in the very climate of the IT industry.

The emergence of computing in the cloud, smart phones and big data mark represent a major technological leap in IT. But it is not just the technology that is changing.

In this age of computing 'in the cloud' the business of IT is changing as fast (if not faster) than the technology. This is clearly evident from changes in today's corporate IT buying decisions.

The people who make today's corporate IT decisions, the basis upon which those decisions are made and the information required — these are among the factors that have undergone radical change. This is both good news and bad news for IT vendors.

Selling IT solutions in the age of the cloud is different to what has gone before. The tools, techniques and frameworks in this book are designed to help sellers to ensure their continued 'rain making' success at this exciting stage in the IT industry's evolution.

Why Read this Book?

In a corporate world of slashed budgets and competing projects selling IT is getting more difficult. The implication for sellers is shown in the image below.

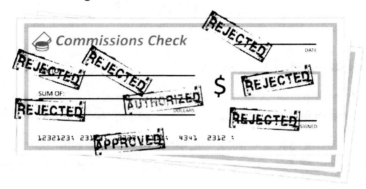

The image above only tells one side of the story however. In particular it does not reveal the underlying problem. The real problem is shown below.

Unless the project, or purchase gets sanctioned there will be no sale. Yet, for every IT project or purchase approved in a large organization there are as many as five or six that are on hold, pending review or face rejection.

That is why this book has been written – that is why it matters. It is written to take the pursuit of the purchase order (PO) to a new level – to bring it more within the control of the salesperson. It has been written to help sellers to unlock and prevent stalled deals.

What New Insights Will You Find?

This book is based on a new insight into why IT buying decisions stall or are scrapped: IT **buying decisions get stalled** not because the buyer cannot choose one supplier over another, but because a compelling business case for the purchase has not been established.

Similarly the reason why one IT vendor loses out to another is not because of price, but because of a more complex business logic, that includes costs, benefits, risk and so on.

These insights into the reality of buying offer new hope to the seller who is faced with stalled or lost deals. They provide the seller with an array of new and even more powerful sales strategies and techniques capable of getting the purchase sanctioned. However it is a radical shift in traditional IT selling.

Who Is this Book for?

This book has been written for all those in pursuit of the IT purchase order. It is primarily aimed at helping IT sales people for whom the PO is the final step of the sale.

However the book does not discriminate between all those for whom the PO is a goal. That is to say it works on both sides of the table – for those buying as well as selling IT. That is no accident given that both sides face the same PO-related challenges of getting important IT projects and purchases approved in an environment of:

- Slashed budgets
- Competing projects
- Greater involvement from Procurement and Finance
- Cross-functional buying teams
- More complex buying processes and procedures.

The frameworks and techniques within this book generate sales commission for IT salespeople. But the source of their power derives from the fact they also help IT directors, IT project managers and others to get their IT projects and purchases approved. After all that is what so many sales commissions depend upon.

What Are the Benefits of this Book?

Selling In The Clouds has been written for you to help your customers and prospects get their projects and purchases approved. In that way it creates a real win-win for both seller and buyer.

Of course it won't help to get every purchase or project approved – that is just not possible. But it will help you to decide early which projects have a realistic chance of success and which ones don't. That means you spend your time backing the real winners.

The payback of this book for the IT salesperson is more POs and higher commissions. For the seller's customers it offers the promise of a higher payback from spending on IT projects and purchases. The business case framework at the core of this book should 'kill off'

IT projects or purchases that are not needed, or won't generate a return for the business. So that means everybody wins and in particular Procurement and Finance should be happy. Its objective is to ensure better IT decisions from a business perspective.

For those IT projects and purchases that get the go ahead, using the framework at the core of this book will help to ensure that they enjoy the maximum chance of success (measured in terms of impact on the performance of the business).

The contents of this book work for those buying, as well as selling, IT. It is about the perfect win-win for both buyer and seller. The buyer cannot buy if a PO is not issued – just as the seller cannot win the sale without it. As the seller, you can help the buyer achieve his or her objectives (the PO) and in turn your own (the sale).

How to Read the Book?

This book is meant to be a practical handbook rather than an academic textbook.

The ideas, tools and frameworks are designed to be put to work – to help you in your everyday sales activities.

The book contains plenty of exercises and tools for you to use. We recommend that you discuss what you read here with your colleagues, challenge it, but most important of all put it to work by applying it to real customers and prospects in your pipeline.

Every time you read a few pages make a note of some actions you can take. Adopt a curious mind-set – try it out. Adapt it to your own products and customers. Find the parts that are most useful for you and your customers.

The test is whether it works for you to help your customers to buy. The experiences of so many other salespeople tell us that it will.

What Makes this Book Different?

This book is aimed at helping IT salespeople to win new friends among IT buyers. In particular it is about the ability to **influence the executives from Procurement and Finance** who play such an important role in today's IT decisions. We like to think of it as the sales equivalent of *How to Win Friends and Influence People* – the classic self-help book written by Dale Carnegie in the 1930s.

Our particular specialism is the implications for sales success of changes in buying. Not surprisingly therefore this book is based on extensive research into how IT and other buying decisions are made.

We are proud to be recognized as being among the leaders globally in terms of our research into how buying decisions are made and in particular the requirements of selling to Procurement and more sophisticated buyers in general.

Why Did We Write this Book?

Here is a paragraph from the book we wrote in 2010:

> *The fundamental importance of business logic or the business case is the iron law of buying. We call it a law because it is fixed and immutable. Its existence does not depend on the seller understanding the need for a business case, or what it should contain. It does not depend on the seller seeing the business case, or even influencing it. The business case is at the center of big buying, whether the salesperson likes it or not.*

The book was called *The B2B Sales Revolution* and it revealed in its full complexity the buying process behind a major IT purchase in a Fortune 1000 corporation. It has been the focus of sales training workshops covering more than 30 different countries.

Given the scope of the research underpinning our first book we had not planned any major changes or a sequel for many years. That was until we uncovered **another set of sweeping changes** in the IT decision-making process. The root cause was the rise of cloud-based IT solutions and services.

In our workshops sales teams work in groups to build the business case for key deals in their pipelines. The business case is **the economic justification** for the purchase decision by the customer. However since 2012 in particular we have noticed a key trend emerging. For salespeople who had spent decades selling traditional IT **the move to the cloud is presenting challenges**.

When you move away from the 'marketing hype' around the cloud sellers struggle to build the business case justification for the purchase of cloud-based *versus* traditional IT solutions. Hence we decided to undertake more research into the buyer's business case for IT in this the age of cloud computing.

Rather than surveying the IT department, we decided to focus on **the view from Finance**. The rationale was as follows:

- We wanted to examine the business decision behind investing in IT because **economics and other factors** are now as important as technical factors in making the decision

- **Finance is increasingly involved** in IT buying decisions, so too are their cousins in Procurement. We wanted their logical-analytical, numbers-driven perspective
- With **pressure on budgets** we wanted to know how to justify the decision from a financial perspective.

What Was the Research Behind the Book?

The research upon which this book is based has four pillars:

- We explored over **150 buying decisions** from the perspective of both the buyer and the seller, including the key decision criteria, steps involved, stakeholders, obstacles to arriving at a decision, internal approvals process and so on
- Most revealing of all we undertook detailed **conversations with a select panel** of financial executives from six big organizations (all except one was a global corporation)
- We reviewed the **present 'state of play'** in respect of IT cloud computing, with a particular focus on:
  - The messages being communicated by IT vendors, based on an extensive review of marketing materials, white papers, webinars and so on
  - The analysis and recommendations of experts based on a review of some of the most popular books recently published on 'computing in the cloud'
- We reviewed and updated concepts and tools that we have been **researching for more than five years**, including many of the tools presented in our earlier books.

How Is the Book Structured?

The book is written in two parts.

Part 1 contains a powerful framework for building the business case. It uses a tried and tested approach that we presented in our 2010 book called **The B2B Sales Revolution**, but this time with a lot more context for the salesperson. That has been added thanks to in-depth interviews with senior financial executives involved in IT buying decisions from 10 large global organizations. Their advice is invaluable to salespeople who find themselves selling to numbers-obsessed buyers.

Part 2 contains a range of insights and strategies to help the seller to get the PO, including:

- Preventing stalled deals **(Chapter 11)**
- How your sales proposal can help get the purchase sanctioned **(Chapter 12)**
- Making your benefits messages more powerful by focusing on business impact **(Chapter 14)**
- The most powerful sales question and the importance of the buyer's definition of success **(Chapter 15)**
- Using numbers and metrics to sell **(Chapter 16)**
- The Total Cost Of Ownership and its role in price negotiations **(Chapter 17)**
- ROI tools that work **(Chapter 18)**
- How factors that complicate the decision can help the salesperson **(Chapter 19)**
- Selling to the buyer's hidden agenda **(Chapter 20)**.

The book is aimed at delivering insights, rather than statistics. In as far as possible it does so using the actual words and expressions of those we interviewed. It is written as a handbook for IT project sponsors and project managers, as well as IT vendors.

Where to Find Out More?

Of course we couldn't cover everything in this book. We had to prioritize those topics and techniques we felt could provide you with the greatest and most immediate sales advantage.

You will find lots more help online at **www.sellingintheclouds.com** and its even richer sister site **www.buyerinsights.com**. That help includes tools and tips on other topics such as setting up or navigating a buying process, managing stakeholders and realizing project benefits.

Part 1

Getting the PO

1: Why Selling 'In The Clouds' Is Different

Introduction

Selling IT in the age of the cloud is different. In an era of tight budgets with projects and technologies competing for resources getting major purchases sanctioned is no easy matter.

Indeed, for every IT project or purchase approved in a large organization there are as many as five or six that are on hold, pending review or simply in a long queue. But unless the project or purchase gets sanctioned there will be no sale. The implications for how vendors sell their solutions are great.

Why Selling IT In the Clouds Is Different

Traditionally vendors emphasized their **competitive advantage**, or **unique selling point** as a means of winning the sale. Competing vendors would therefore 'slug it out' over benefits, features and reputation. Today that is no longer adequate as a basis for sales success.

In an environment of slashed budgets, the real battle is not selecting the best supplier, but accessing the budget or getting internal approval. The real battle is not between competing vendors, but between competing projects, priorities and strategies.

Selling IT in the age of the cloud is different. That is because buying IT has changed.

Today the IT vendor's proposal must help the IT manager or sponsor to secure budget, to justify the decision and to get it sanctioned. Projects that cannot be justified based on their numbers are at risk of being stalled, or scrapped. Faced with these new realities the seller must help the buyer to build the business case justification for the project or purchase.

Buying IT Has Changed

Buying IT has changed. The implications for how IT is sold are profound. They work on four levels as shown in the table below.

The Implications for Selling IT of Changes In Buying

Key Dimensions of Selling IT	How IT Was Sold Traditionally	Selling IT In 'The Age Of The Cloud'
1. Who needs to be persuaded	IT executives	Cross-functional buying teams, including Procurement and Finance
2. What they need to be persuaded of	Technical superiority of our solution over competitors'	Delivers the results the business wants and the best value
3. How to persuade them	Showing how our solution matches the customer's needs	Building the business case justification (including costs & benefits, risk & compliance)
4. Who / What is the competition	The competition is another vendor	The competition is another purchase, project or priority. It is also a decision to do nothing, to delay a decision, or to do in-house

Although your customers are likely to be found at different stages of the journey from 'old IT' to 'new IT' the overall direction of movement is unmistakable. Everywhere there is more rigorous control of organizational spending and the professionalization of buying in respect of IT products and services.

Let's examine how the changes in buying have impacted on each of the four key dimensions of IT selling.

IT Sales Dimension 1: Who Needs to be Persuaded

Traditional selling IT involved convincing the IT manager or sponsor about the technological superiority of one solution over another. This is still important and always will be. But it is not enough in an environment where IT buying decisions are no longer dominated by technical considerations, or indeed made by technical people.

In the past managers of IT departments had a significant level of autonomy over spending decisions, including the selection of a preferred vendor and solution. However, those decisions are now increasingly governed by procurement procedures and cross-functional buying committees. The salesperson must now sell to a wider business audience and a diversity of stakeholders.

The increased involvement of Procurement and Finance in so many IT spending decisions adds greatly to the complexity of the sale. One thing is clear from the research published in this book: financial executives have a very different take on IT decisions to their IT colleagues.

IT managers must be able to justify the decision if the purchase or project is to be sanctioned and budget secured. What is required is a rational-economic justification and this book is about the framework for sellers to help buyers to create it.

IT Sales Dimension 2: What Do They Need to be Persuaded of

The mark of an excellent vendor proposal used to be that it 'blew the competition out of the water'. But, today more is needed if the PO is to be certain.

Today's IT decisions are heavily swayed by business rather than technical considerations. That is no surprise given the emergence of the 'new buyer' in respect of IT. Decisions regarding IT products and projects are no longer the sole preserve of IT executives. Increasingly those involved in shaping and making the decision don't know PHP, Java or even HTML. Being from Finance, Procurement and other departments they don't need to.

Today's new IT buyers know more about business than they do about technology. Little wonder then that IT decisions increasingly resemble other business decisions or that the focus has moved from technology to payback.

Today's vendor proposal needs to do more that sell a technology if it is going to persuade Procurement and Finance. It has to justify the decision – to show a clear business justification for the project or purchase.

This book has been written to help you to sell IT projects and purchases to non-IT people in a way that wins approvals and releases budgets. It marks an exciting expansion in the role of the seller.

The frameworks and techniques in this book build upon sellers' existing sales skills and techniques. They add another layer of sophistication in order to enable sellers to meet the challenges of getting the PO in the modern corporate Procurement-led environment. This additional layer of skills is aimed at getting POs that might otherwise fall through the seller's hands.

The business case behind any purchase is based on fact, logic and analysis. It demands a new form of selling – one that replaces the sales pitch with a spreadsheet, marketing with metrics, influence with insights and persuasion with logic.

IT Sales Dimension 3: How to Persuade Them

Today's IT decisions are becoming more like business decisions. That is to say they are subject to greater scrutiny – they are more hard-nosed and numbers-driven. Often the main stakeholder is no longer the IT department itself.

Increasingly there is a 'new buyer' in the form of Procurement, Finance and other departments. The challenge is that these new buyers think differently. In general they are less interested in features and more interested in benefits.

Indeed for 'the new buyer' the technology is often only the means to an end. The technology is a secondary need – the primary need is to save time or money, gain a competitive edge, win over customers and so on.

Increasingly today's IT decision revolves around what the technology will enable the customer to achieve – the impact on the performance of a task, project, function or facility. That makes it as much a business decision as a technology decision.

The locus of the decision has changed. This presents challenges for IT managers and vendors for whom the technology is still the primary focus.

IT Sales Dimension 4: Who / What is the Competition

Traditionally salespeople feared losing the deal to a competing vendor. However, this is only one of the threats in the modern IT procurement environment. The competition for purchase is another purchase, project or priority. It is also a decision to do nothing, to delay a decision, or to do in-house.

The reality is that sales people are not the only ones who have funnels; buyers have them too! Let's turn to the IT director of a large multinational to explain:

> Last year we had 300 million worth of projects for consideration across the organization, but only a budget of 100 million. That meant we were faced with some very hard choices and they were choices between projects and even departments, not choices between suppliers.

It is a classic funnel scenario, lots of IT projects and proposals go in at the top, but only a small proportion emerge successfully at the bottom, in terms of sanctioned expenditure, approved budgets and signed purchase orders. Clearly, buyers have funnels too!

What are the implications of the buyer funnel? Well, salespeople know to their cost that many projects never get 'off the ground' and they know that projects can fall even at the last hurdle. At the core of why decisions get scrapped and stalled is the issue of the buyer's funnel and the rules that govern it.

Again here is the IT director's description of the process:

> With a large portfolio of projects chasing limited funds for investment, the choices, trade-offs and compromises are difficult. We have to make a calculated decision as to which projects will survive and which ones won't based on the business case.
>
> The business case is king and its preparation demands rigorous analysis and preparation by a cross-functional team. You have to have people on side, but you also have to have the numbers backing it up.

The challenge of gaining approval for a project or purchase is a shared one for the buyer and the seller. Manager-buyers must sell their projects and purchases internally if they are to succeed. That makes them salespeople in their own right and in turn it makes the salesperson's commission dependent on the manager's ability to sell.

Sellers Depend on the Sales Skills of the Buyer

The reality of modern buying is that the seller is rarely in the room when the decision is finally made. All too often the decision on an IT project or purchase is made behind closed doors and involves a committee-type meeting and a long trail of paper.

The IT salesperson can do a great job in selling his or her solution. But that is not enough – the executives on the other side of the table (in the customer organization) must do a great job too.

The **sales person's commission is often dependent on the IT manager being able to sell their projects and purchases internal**ly – to get the approval of Procurement and Finance for example.

It is a scary reality – the seller's success dependent on the sales skills of the IT executive! The only way to make it less scary is for the salesperson to get more actively involved in helping the buyer to justify the decision.

Today the IT vendor's proposal must help the IT manager or sponsor in the buying organization to:

- Loosen purse strings
- Win budgets and resources
- Align stakeholders
- Fend off competing projects
- Prevent stalled decisions
- Navigate buying processes and procedures.

If the seller is going to do any of these things then he or she must help the IT manager to justify the decision and to get it sanctioned. That means the salesperson has to help the customer to build a compelling business case for the IT project or purchase. In the next chapter we begin our exploration of what the business case for IT really is and why it is so powerful.

2: The Business Case for IT

Introduction

In this chapter we illuminate the factors that are involved in the decision to invest in IT, both cloud-based and traditional. Importantly, we will do this not just from a technology, but a business, point of view.

To put it another way, we are going to build the business case, or **justification for IT**, in the age of cloud computing. But don't let that stop you reading (especially if you see your role as selling technology solutions).

The Rise of the Business Case

The level of **business logic and rigor applied to IT decisions** varies from organization to organization. Yet, in most organizations there is a trend towards the increased sophistication of IT decision-making.

Businesses are spending large amounts of money on IT and that spending is **coming under increased scrutiny**. As with any business investment a logical-analytical appraisal of IT spending decisions must be undertaken. In other words some form of business case justification is required.

Increasingly the decision around IT is being shaped not by the merits of the technology, but by **the needs of the business**. There are five trends that put the business case at the core of IT decisions:

- **Slashed budgets** – with budget cuts organization-wide, spending decisions in IT, as in other areas, must be justified

- **Competing projects** – in most organizations there are more IT projects and purchases than there are funds available to finance them. Projects must compete on their merits for funding and some projects will win, while others will lose.

Ideally the most compelling business case should secure funding

- **Involvement of Procurement** – there is a trend toward greater professionalism and sophistication in buying IT, with increased involvement by Procurement and Finance. The IT manager's discretion regarding suppliers and purchases has been curtailed

- **Governance, Risk and Compliance (GRC)** – given the importance of IT to the business it is a key element of good corporate governance, risk management and compliance. Failure to properly manage IT could have major financial, legal and other consequences for the business. It could even threaten the organization's future

- **Competitive pressures** – IT plays an important role in delivering on those business strategies needed to respond to changing market conditions. Investments in IT are expected to deliver upon the need for increased competitiveness, efficiency and innovation.

Managers who want to get their IT projects or purchases approved can think of the business case as the ultimate 'killer app'. It has the power to ensure project success – whether that is getting the project off the ground, securing budget, accessing resources, managing expectations or aligning stakeholders.

There Is No Getting Away from 'The Business Case'

There is simply no getting away from the business case when it comes to dealing with today's buyers. Here are four examples of the pervasiveness of the business case we witnessed in just one week as we were writing this book:

- A meeting to fast-track the implementation of a new CRM system was stalled when one senior manager asked not about supplier selection or system specifications but rather about the business case. The question was met with an embarrassed silence and it was back to the drawing board, with all those attending the meeting agreeing that taking any steps before the business case had been reviewed was, in their own words, 'putting the cart before the horse'

- Finding it difficult to choose between two options put forward by the short-listed vendor, the buying team in a public body found a novel way to break the impasse. They asked the seller to prepare a business case for selecting its more expensive Option A, over a cheaper Option B. Specifically, they wanted the seller's recommendation in the form of a no-nonsense costs, benefits and risk equation

- The salesperson was preparing for an important call with a prospect that he was eager to progress to the next stage of the sales cycle. He reviewed the notes of previous meetings and in his mind played out the different ways that the call could go. Then after writing out some points to guide the conversation, he tested the sales pitch out on a colleague. The colleague listened intensively but was unimpressed. He suggested a better approach – directly address the cost, benefits and risks for the prospect in moving to the next stage of the sales process. That put the focus on the logic for the buyer of investing more time in engaging with the seller

- 'I can kiss the VP promotion goodbye if this project does not work out' exclaimed the manager-buyer in a global corporation. This points to the fact that the business case is not just cold business logic, but has also has a strong personal dimension. The cost / benefits / risk equation of the business case must be applied on a personal, as well as on a commercial, level.

So, what do these anecdotes mean for the seller? Well, they mean that he or she had better share the buyer's obsession for the business case, putting it at the core of their selling.

What Is the Business Case?

The nature of today's IT decisions requires getting familiar with some new terminology. That includes **language that was once the preserve of the accountant or CEO**. However, don't let any of these new terms intimidate you. For those experienced in communicating complex technical information, terms such as business case, investment decision and economic justification will prove relatively easy to grasp.

The term 'business case' as it is used in this book is **'the justification required for any IT project or purchase to secure funds or to win approval'**. We are taking a very literal interpretation: Business case = **the case for the business** to make a particular IT strategy, project, or purchase decision.

Our interpretation in this book of the 'business case' is a fluid one. It recognizes that the requirements of approval vary from company to company and even between different IT products or services within the same company. For example the requirements for getting a PO issued for the purchase of 12 new software licenses or cloud service subscriptions is likely to be different from that for a new CRM or ERP solution.

What matters to the salesperson is finding out the requirements of approval for each sales opportunity in the pipeline. In doing so this book will provide the tools that the seller needs. In particular it will provide a universal framework for the IT business case justification that can be adapted to the specific requirement of any pipeline opportunity.

What The Business Case Is Not

Because you are going to see the term 'business case' or 'business case justification' used a lot in this book it is worth spending a moment considering in more detail what it is and what it is not.

The term business case means different things to different people, including the following interpretations:

- '… a document, sometimes a big one …'
- '… something that an accountant, bank manager or investor would want'
- '… a bureaucratic procedure or form to be completed'
- '… a way of justifying a decision, a project, or a purchase'
- '… the application of logic to how a decision is made'
- '… a tool for getting a project / decision passed'
- '… a mechanism used to stall, delay or frustrate a decision'
- '… a folly given that most decisions are made emotionally!'.

When people hear the word business case they sometimes get a confused look. They start wondering about 'what goes in it?', 'what size it should be?', 'who writes it?' and so on. But the business case is **best viewed as an argument or a process, rather than a document**. It is better considered as a rationale rather than a report.

Of course the business case often ends up as a document. But whether it ends up as a five, 15 or 50 page document, whether it takes two days or 12 months to prepare and regardless of whether it is signed off by the CEO, the board, or simply a line manager – all these are secondary to the role of the business case as the analytical means for arriving at or justifying a decision.

The Logical Rational Decision

For those who have studied business, almost at any level, business logic and the business case should be something very familiar. It is the application of Business 101 principles: in other words business decisions should be made to maximize (long-term) economic return.

Managers have a responsibility to their shareholders — to grow profits, revenue and asset values. This requires the application of hard-nosed business logic to **all** business decisions, including those relating to IT projects and purchases. It also requires decision-making that is based on good information, analysis and planning.

IT requires a logical-analytical basis for the decision – that is the business case. It is a basis on which a manager will decide – weighing up different factors involved: cost and benefits, risks, how it fits with other decisions / strategies and so on. That is the theory, but in reality for some buyers the business case may be used to justify be a decision that has already been made.

Although it can be seen as generating additional work for the manager who previously could simply make the decision and get on with their job, the business case can serve the manager too. The business case is a means of risk insurance for the manager who does not want to 'go out on a limb' or risk getting it wrong.

A Formula for the Business Case

Commonsense tells us that the decision in respect of important IT projects and purchases has much in common with any other investment decision. It follows therefore that the business case for cloud computing or traditional software or hardware follows the same structure as the business case for any other form of business investment.

Most business investment decisions follow a predictable pattern. Indeed, so much so that the factors involved in the decision can be grouped under five headings:

- Economics (or cost / benefits)
- Risk
- Compliance
- Strategic fit
- Politics.

Using these five headings the fundamental underlying business case for any IT investment can be calculated using the following formula:

This equation is the basis for building the business case justification either for or against an IT investment in the clouds. It is what gets projects approved and purchase orders generated.

The formula is based on the analysis of a real world *Fortune 500* IT investment decision and was first published in **The B2B Sales Revolution** (2010).

Obviously, this is a **business, rather than a technology, equation**. So while technical issues such as security, performance and flexibility are included they are principally addressed from a business, rather than an IT, perspective.

Since it was first published in 2010, this business case equation has been used to build and validate thousands of business cases for solutions ranging from IT investments to large scale construction projects. More to the point it has been used to build a **compelling reason to buy IT – to accelerate some IT projects, while killing off others**.

One of the reasons why the business case equation has proven so popular (and indeed so powerful) is because it acts as an effective **decision simplification strategy**. That is to say it enables the sponsor or seller to bring the conversation back to the very basics of the decision. In other words it is aimed at answering the question: 'Why should we buy or invest in this hardware, software or cloud-based application?'.

In building out the business case formula (as shown above) we asked a cross-section of CFOs and other financial executives to share their views on the business case for 'IT in the cloud'. We wanted to put the focus on the financial executive who is so often involved in today's IT decisions.

The objective is to help those making IT decisions, as well as those selling IT solutions. It is aimed at informing the argument both for and against cloud computing, providing a framework for the business decision-making process and a means by which the seller can influence the business decision behind the technology sale.

> Most traditional selling is based on **relationships, persuasion and influence**. It is not that these factors are redundant in selling to today's more numbers-driven buyer – it is just that they are not enough.

The New 'Gold Standard' for IT Decisions

The business case is the 'gold standard' for important IT buying decisions. It is the way decisions should be made. But it would be dangerous to assume that it is always achieved.

Any IT decision should be capable of **standing up to scrutiny** – it should be backed up by an analysis that is fact-based and numbers-rich. IT requires a clear business case justification – that is what the management textbooks and best practice principles say. However in reality this is not always the case, which presents an opportunity and a challenge for the salesperson.

Sellers should **not assume that every IT project or purchase has a business case**, or at least one that is sufficiently robust. This is clear from all our research. In particular don't assume that the numbers make sense. For example they may have been pulled together to justify a decision that has already been made and so they may lack any objective external validation.

Our research shows that the reality of IT decision-making **often falls short of what might be expected**. However if those in Finance have their way that won't be tolerated for much longer. Projects that don't have a supporting business case are increasingly being weeded out and 'stopped in their tracks'. Sellers need to help the buyer to ensure that the logic of the decision is clear – that the business case is compelling.

Business Case = Powerful Sales Tool

For the seller the business case is **a powerful sales tool** – it can be used at all stages of the sale, but most importantly in advancing or closing the deal. It is simply a way for the seller to structure the argument for buying his or her solution in a manner that will have maximum impact on the sophisticated or professional buyer. Well at least it should be. The reality however is that the business case is as underused as it is powerful.

Sellers only have **information on the buyer's business case** for every second deal. That is based on research we did with B2B salespeople who are involved in up to 43,000 deals a year.

The business case is the road less travelled when it comes to selling IT. In as many as five out of 10 deals (or 53% to be exact) the salesperson did **not** have access to the following important information:

- The essentials of the buyer's **business case** rationale for the purchase
- The key **metrics** of interest to the buyer to sell our solution
- Information required to calculate / present a **payback** to the buyer.

The implication is that salespeople are failing to develop or to use **the most powerful argument for the purchase** of their solution. This can happen in many ways:

- The focus is on the competitive advantages of the supplier, rather than the **business results** that the solution can help the buyer achieve
- Benefits are not **quantified,** or not subjected to third party validation
- The price does not address the lifetime cost, or **total cost of ownership**
- There is no **ROI,** or one that has little credibility for the buyer
- **Risks** (including supplier risk, project risk) or Key Success Factors are not addressed.

If any of the above applies to the deals in your pipeline then the good news is that there is a powerful sales strategy available to you. It is to help the buyer to build the business case.

Not knowing the buyer's business case handicaps the seller in any number of ways. It limits the seller's ability to accurately forecast the likelihood and timing of the deal and effectively to prequalify the opportunity. It also hinders the seller in price negotiations and in particular in moving the conversation off price and onto value. Most important of all it means that the seller is missing vital leverage in closing the sale.

> *The business case is the nexus of the purchase, or buying decision. That means it is should also be the focus of the sale. However, in most cases it is not. Indeed, the business case is one of the most powerful, yet under-utilized sales techniques or strategies available to the seller.*

Selling to the business case can present challenges for the seller. However if you stick with it you will be rewarded. Indeed it could be the most rewarding struggle you've had for a long time.

Our research suggests that sellers who engage with their customers to build a compelling business case can **boost closing success by anywhere from 5% to 25%**. So, with that promise in mind, let's set about building the business case starting with the economics of the IT project, or purchase.

> *Without reference to the business case the salesperson, sales pitch and sales proposal focus on secondary issues such as features and benefits of their product / solution, and their company's competitive advantages, rather than the primary issue of what they can help the buyer achieve. The seller is focused on adjectives and marketing prose, rather than the economic rationale or algebra of the business case.*

3: Economics 'In The Clouds'

Introduction

Obviously the decision around IT in the clouds is going to be numbers-driven. It is **a rational-economic decision**, based on the analysis of costs and benefits. That is clearly the perspective of the financial executives we spoke to.

The cost / benefits analysis in respect of IT however is not as straightforward as it sounds. Indeed, the term itself means different things to different people.

First there is the **marketing interpretation** of cost and benefits, reflected in the language typically found in the sales presentations and web pages of vendors. Below is an example of how a typical SaaS solution sells itself:

- Easy to setup, configure and support:
  - Get into production in minutes rather than weeks or months
  - Remove dependency on IT staff
  - No software downloads or plug-ins required
  - Allows companies to focus on core business
- OPex *versus* CAPex – control your costs:
  - Easy to setup, configure and support
  - Get into production in minutes rather than weeks or months
  - Remove dependency on IT staff
  - No software downloads or plug-ins required
  - Allows companies to focus on core business.

Benefits Minus Cost

Not surprisingly, given that those we interviewed had financial background, the term 'cost / benefits' has **a more strict economic meaning**. It is something that goes beyond marketing speak – it is about benefits minus cost. Moreover it is the first (and arguably the most important) part of the business case.

Not surprisingly, the view from Finance is that the cost and benefits of IT projects and purchases must be quantified. Indeed it must be monetized and capable of being expressed in context of the key financial reports of the business:

- The income statement / P&L
- The cash flow statement
- The balance sheet.

These are the three reports that matter to Finance and indeed to the business. So, if the justification for investing in IT is to be credible it must be expressed in terms of its impact on each. That is, its impact on profitability, liquidity and the financial structure of the business.

These issues are addressed later in this book, but first it is important to set the background – to recap on the recent history of the business case for IT.

The New IT Investment Model

The IT investment decision can be among **the most difficult of decisions**. That is something that quickly becomes clear, both in conversations with financial executives, as well as buyers and sellers of IT.

Exactly how IT decisions should be made is something that has been debated for a long time. At the peak of the debate a number of influential books were published on how to calculate, manage and justify IT expenditure and investment.

Little could the authors of those books have anticipated that in less than a decade so much of what they had written would be out-of-date. With the advent of 'IT in the cloud' **the IT investment decision has been transformed**.

The IT Investment Decision Transformed

Traditionally the bucket of IT costs included:

- Hardware costs
- Software costs
- Licenses
- Integration
- Installation
- Commissioning
- Customization
- Testing.

Many of these costs were incurred at the outset of a project, often representing **a sizeable capital outlay** – perhaps hundreds of thousands, if not millions, of dollars or euros. This investment would be paid back over a number of years, with the return on investment becoming an important aspect of justifying the decision.

Although the initial upfront investment (and in particular the ticket price) generally gets most attention, it was typically only part of **the total cost equation**. Other costs included:

- Internal project resources
- Training
- Administration
- System maintenance and support
- Help desk support to users
- Energy and other running costs.

These costs were typically not paid up front, but were associated with the **implementation, maintenance and operation** of the IT solution. They appeared in the income statement or P&L under a diversity of headings, including IT staff costs, electricity and facilities costs.

As IT evolved through the decades these operating costs have tended to grow as a proportion of the total lifecycle cost. Over the past decade it was not unusual that they would match, or even exceed, the initial hardware or software investment. Indeed, in many cases the purchase price of the software or hardware represents only the tip of the iceberg.

The Iceberg Principle and Total Cost of Ownership

The iceberg principle is a powerful metaphor for your customer's Total Cost of Ownership (TCO). It suggests that, just like an iceberg, much of the bulk of the buyer's total cost may not be obvious.

While the price of the solution is plain to see, it may account for only a relatively small proportion of the customer's total cost.

There are costs that are often hidden and they can dwarf the purchase price. Such costs might include:

- Internal time and resources
- Overheads
- Expenses
- Opportunity cost.

The list of possible costs that make up TCO is endless – so it is important to determine the specific costs for your project, or purchase. You will find more on TCO in **Chapter 17** in **Part 2**.

It is in respect of total cost of ownership that many mistakes in respect of buying IT have been made. In particular, it is all too easy to underestimate what an IT project will really costs. This is a problem that cloud computing can address.

A New Era Begins

The advent of cloud computing turned the traditional IT investment model on its head. It replaced major up front expenditures with monthly 'all-inclusive' 'pay as you go' subscriptions. The result is that the three to five year IT payback model is now redundant! Or is it?

To explore this question let's begin by discussing the 'benefits minus cost' part of the cloud IT business case equation.

Calculating IT Cost – A New Level of Science

While calculating the benefits of IT in the clouds may still be a challenge, there would appear to be little doubt that cloud computing **has made calculating cost easier**. Here is how one executive put it:

> I can go on to Amazon web services for example and calculate the cost with a surprising degree of accuracy. They have turned the art of budgeting for IT provision into a science. Knowing with confidence what you have to spend has real appeal to the budget holder.

The advent of **'accurate to the penny'** costs in respect of cloud computing is a welcome change 'in an industry with a history of unpredictable and rising costs'. This is a point emphasized by a number of executives from Finance.

> 'Most IT project budgets are already in the clouds' joked one cynical CFO. He went on to explain that when it comes to projecting the cost and payback for new IT projects many managers 'have their heads in the clouds'.

There was a serious point behind the pun: 'There is simply not enough rigor in the analysis or accuracy around the numbers. The result is that cost over-runs are common' added the CFO.

As we will see in **Chapter 6** predictability around cost is something that executives may be prepared to pay more for.

While many argue that accurately calculating IT cost has become easier, the same cannot be said in respect to calculating the benefits.

Calculating the Benefits

Many financial executives will suggest that in spite of the new model of cloud computing 'the most important part of the business case for IT remains unchanged'. That is the payback to the business and that is the part that is hardest to quantify, validate, or track.

Calculating the benefits of IT is not easy, ask any accountant! The challenges involved include calculating money saved, costs avoided and of course revenues generated. Perhaps the key word here is 'calculating', as the requirement is to quantify (in a monetary sense) the benefits.

True to their accounting background, several of the financial executives pointed out that **benefits that are not (or cannot be) quantified** are relatively 'meaningless'. Here are some of the points raised:

> Of all the aspects of the cost / benefits equation with which the buyer will struggle, the one that poses the greatest challenge is the calculation of the **impact on the key metrics** of the business, the project, or the team. That is the case whether the customer is paying for hardware and licenses under the traditional model, or based on the new cloud business model.

> The central question remains how will the money spent on IT impact on the performance of the business and how can it be measured. The business case for cloud versus traditional IT comes second to the business case for IT, full stop. That is an obvious point – but one that is easily overlooked!

The implication appears to be that whether you are in favor of, or against, computing in the clouds, the place to start is the benefits to the business. But this is an area with which many organizations are likely to be struggling.

In our conversations Finance executives were putting their colleagues from IT and other departments on notice. They were spelling out **the need for a rock-solid analysis of the benefits** of the IT investment (in the clouds, or otherwise).

What Are Hard Savings?

Clouds may be soft and fluffy, but when it comes to calculating the benefits of an investment in IT (whether in the clouds or not), financial executives draw a clear distinction between hard and soft savings.

Hard savings are tangible and concrete – they can be tracked in the financial reports. They are reductions in:

- Office and administration costs
- Energy and communication costs
- Raw material costs
- Cost of production
- Manpower costs
- Sales and marketing costs.

Many managers talk about 'hard savings' as being savings that have been quantified, but that may not be enough. A 'hard saving' can be **tracked in the financial statements** of the company. They can be compared from year to year using historical spend data.

It is important to recognize that 'not all savings are equal'. If you want to get and keep the attention of executives in Finance, hard savings are where to begin. This applies to traditional as well as cloud-based IT decisions.

What Are Soft Savings?

Most arguments for spending on IT fall into the realm not of hard, but soft, savings. But that can present problems in justifying the spend decision.

Soft savings are less tangible. Typically they are realized from not spending money, or by saving time and other resources.

Common soft savings are as follows:

- Improved cash flow and reduced working capital requirements
- Avoidance of costs that could otherwise have been incurred
- Preventing a price increase from a supplier
- Getting more from a supplier for the same money (free training, or support)
- A purchase price that is lower than the original quoted price
- Long-term contracts with price-protection provisions
- Intangibles such as improved safety, increased employee motivation, or customer satisfaction and their direct / indirect impact on costs.

Finance departments tend to take a **cynical view of 'soft savings'** claims, treating them (in the words of one CFO) as 'coulda shoulda woulda savings'.

Soft savings are often future or scenario-based and that means tracking them between income statements may be difficult. The **lack of a historical cost data** means that from an accounting point of view a reduction from one period to another cannot be shown.

When savings are soft they are technically **more 'cost avoidance' than 'cost saving'**. Quantifying cost avoidance is challenging and from the perspective of traditional financial statements is often considered relatively meaningless.

As one executives told us, 'Don't be surprised if your savings claims meet with skepticism that is unless they are real or hard savings'.

The hardline 'hard savings' message was tempered by some executives who suggest that 'soft savings' should not be discounted completely. Issues of risk, strategic fit, or compliance can make soft savings compelling. It is just that, in the words of one executive; 'they **will need some convincing**'.

Total cost of ownership, for example, often involves a mix of both hard and soft savings. But if soft savings are to be counted then the project sponsor or salesperson is going to need to make them both credible and compelling.

4: Calculating the Benefits of IT

Calculating
benefits

$ € ¥ £
$ € ¥ £
$ € ¥ £

www.SellingintheClouds.com

Introduction

IT budgets and saving are subject to increased scrutiny. But are the benefits you are communicating compelling enough to get your IT project or purchase approved? That is the question that this chapter has been written to answer.

The promises made by IT projects have not always been realized. Calculations regarding the benefits to the business, or the cost of the project have not always been accurate.

The problem is that while listing the benefits of an IT project or purchase is easy, calculating those benefits is not. Indeed, putting meaningful and credible numbers around the benefits can be a real challenge. That applies to cloud-based, as well as traditional, IT decisions.

IT managers require a new level of numeracy if they are to grapple successfully with business case or cost / benefits analysis for their projects and purchases. They must be able to anticipate the questions and objections that are likely to arise when they are called upon to justify their decision.

In this chapter we identify nine key questions – the answers to which will reveal just how compelling the benefits of any IT project or purchases will be.

Cheaper in the Clouds? Not Necessarily!

In the last chapter we saw how cloud computing makes calculating costs easier, but do people really expect cloud-based services to be cheaper?

Well according to our conversations with Finance, some do while many others do not. More to the point, it is clear that for many **the**

decision is not necessarily about price! There is much more to the numbers debate than you might suspect.

There are a range of factors that determine what benefits will motivate a decision and what benefits won't. While cloud computing often claims the high ground in terms of cost advantages, there are many questions to be asked before the economics of any project can be proven.

How Benefits Are Interrogated

Most IT projects find themselves in a queue, surrounded by a variety of other competing projects and purchases. While they all offer some form of savings promise, most won't be compelling enough to sway a decision. Some benefits are more important than others and central to this is how they are calculated.

The benefit claimed by IT projects and their sponsors or sellers are typically viewed with skepticism and subjected to scrutiny. However the process by which benefits are interrogated is quite predictable. That is important because it means that project sponsors can prepare in advance for the questions or objections that are likely to arise.

Nine Questions that Determine Success

IT projects and their promised benefits are subject to a barrage of questions aimed at separating winning projects from all of the rest. They are the questions used to put project sponsors and managers 'on the spot' – to test their confidence and credibility.

Below we list the nine most commonly asked questions used in order to test or validate a project's cost / benefits analysis. If these questions can be answered with confidence the likelihood of gaining approval for, or successfully justifying, your IT project or purchase is greatly increased.

The nine questions that are used to determine which projects will actually get approved and funded are:

- What overhead costs will actually be reduced?
- What savings can justifiably be claimed?
- What budget will the costs / savings come out of?
- What is the time period involved?
- Is there certainty around costs?
- Are there economies of scale?
- How will it impact on the income statement / P&L?
- What is the 'economic tipping point' (where sunk costs are no longer a barrier)?
- How will it impact on the balance sheet and cash flow?

You can use these questions to gauge how ready you are to justify or seek approval for your project. So, we recommend that you answer each question – just as you would if it was being asked by a colleague in Finance or Procurement. Pay particular attention to those questions that you struggle to answer confidently – they may represent barriers to the success of your project.

How many people need to know the answers to these questions? That is an important point to consider because the project manager or sponsor may not always be present when the project is being discussed. For example, what would happen if your project were to come up for discussion at a senior management meeting where the issue of spending cuts was to be discussed? If somebody else is presenting your project for approval or review then they must be able to answer these questions.

What Overheads Actually Will Be Cut?

If your project is claiming to reduce salaries, or other fixed costs, you will need to be prepared. That is because IT projects that promise a reduction in overheads tend to come in for particular scrutiny. Most managers have learned that promised savings in overheads can be slow to materialize.

As you know costs are typically classified as either fixed or variable. Fixed costs are quite literally fixed– they don't go up or down in direct relationship to sales (or other variables, such as number of users, or a particular period of time). Instead they jump in steps, for example the infrastructure costs may be fixed at $500,000 for the first 1 million users and then jump to $1.3 million for the next 250,000 users. The term 'overhead' is commonly used for those fixed costs, such as salaries, office costs, light and electricity, and so on that are associated with the running of a business, department or project.

Additional costs usually are not a problem if they are associated with increased revenue or other success-related variables. However, if costs jump up in large fixed amounts the question is whether the results will follow.

Therein lies the challenge in forecasting fixed costs. They will be incurred even if user numbers, usage volumes, or revenues fail to reach the projected levels. In that way they are a financial penalty to be paid in respect of the project that underperforms. As a result many managers would be prepared to replace fixed costs with variable costs, in particular for high-risk projects.

Overhead is, in the words of one Finance executive, 'stubborn'. While it can ratchet up quickly, it tends to reduce at a much slower pace. It tends to ratchet up much more predictably than it ratchets down. This is because it may involve people being laid off, the renegotiation of contracts, changing premises or other facilities. This is an important consideration where IT projects promise savings in the form of lower overheads, such as reduced wages, lower facilities costs and so on.

A scenario-based approach to forecasting fixed costs may be useful – for example, addressing the implications of a 3% or 5% increase or decrease in key variables, such as:

- The number of users or volume of usage
- The time required (implications of the 'go live' date being delayed by one month)
- The revenues earned or financial contributions made
- The costs incurred, especially in areas such as integration, roll-out or implementation
- Key variables such as level of support, training or functionality required by users.

The view appears to be that in most organizations **overhead, budgets and manpower can be slow to change**. That is due to the presence of existing commitments, legacy systems and sunk costs, as well as a range of fixed costs and overheads.

Cloud-based computing often promises a leaner approach to IT, in particular reducing IT support and administration costs. However, there appears to be caution among executives in forecasting aggressive savings in this area.

Most suspect that 'there won't be massive downsizing in the face of cloud computing' but rather a more gradual transition and **quite a degree of overlap** at the start.

The key question according to another executive is '**will the IT department shrink** as a result of putting a service in the clouds?'.

The question was a rhetorical one, with the answer being: 'What tends to happen is that IT staff get redirected to other projects, rather than the payroll being reduced. IT managers are naturally protective of their departments, head-counts and budgets'.

So, for political and other reasons, savings claimed in these areas need to be treated with caution – this is examined in **Chapters 8** and **9**.

Putting It To Work

What aspects of overhead are likely to be reduced and how quickly? Use the table below to answer this question.

Fast or Immediate Overhead Reduction	Slow or Long-term Overhead Reduction

What Savings Justifiably Can Be Claimed?

As discussed earlier not all savings are credible or compelling. Just how powerful they are depends on how many of the following four criteria apply:

- Quantified (can be calculated)
- Monetized (calculated in dollars or euro)
- Hard rather than soft (relate to a historical cost line)
- Linked to the financial statements (the income statement or P&L).

Putting It To Work

To see just how compelling the savings claims for an IT solution (cloud-based or not) are, use the following table to check how many of the above criterion have been met.

	Tick If Present
Quantified (can be calculated)	
Monetized (calculated in dollars, or euro)	
Hard rather than soft (relate to a historical cost line)	
Linked to the financial statements (the income statement or P&L)	

We sat in on 50 randomly-chosen vendor pitches last July and here is what we found:

- 90% plus of the benefits communicated were simply verbalized
- Less than 10% of them had any quantification of benefits.

The power of communicating benefits that comply with the criteria shown in the table above in part derives from the fact that it is rarely done.

Whose Budget Will Be Affected?

'Whose budget will it affect?' That is probably one of the most important questions that project sponsors and sellers should ask. It is important to consider such factors as:

- Has a budget been allocated for this project?
- Is there one overall budget or several contributors?

- Has the budget been ring-fenced, or could it be redirected to another area?
- What percentage of the total budget / spend in the area does this purchase / project account for?
- Are there pressures on the budget? (Is spend ahead or behind target? Is the budget growing, or shrinking?)
- What is the overhead or headcount associated with the budget, in terms of project management, administration, etc?
- What KPIs, metrics or reports will the project impact on?
- How much control or scrutiny is there of the budget?
- Who, if anybody, will be rewarded (or rebuked) based on what is spent, or what is saved?
- Will the spend come from the IT budget, or that of an end user department, or function?
- Who ultimately signs the check? Who has the power to increase, or allocate the budget?

The test for the salesperson is to answer the above questions with confidence. However, the answers may not be as straightforward as they at first seem. Some of the reasons why are explained below.

One skeptical executive suggested that in respect of most projects and departments **there are two forces at play**: those driving towards protecting and increasing spend, and those striving to reduce it. Quite simply there are some people for whom spending less may not be an objective.

Managers may not be very interested in savings unless they impact on the **variables by which they are measured, or incentivized**. In the context of their own performance metrics, cost savings in respect of the IT systems used may not be an important factor. For example a cost saving means little if it increases the risk of a system being unavailable or puts data security at risk.

Finding what budget the IT project should come out of is a major factor in determining the pace at which a project will advance. For example where there are multiple stakeholders and various departments that are expected to contribute budget there can be challenges in getting agreement as to **'how the bill is to be split'**.

In this respect the 'metered' basis on which the cost of computing in the clouds has an advantage. Paying for IT based on usage and in a very transparent way can be attractive to many managers and their departments.

What Time Period Is Involved?

A challenge faced by traditional IT investments is the longer-term payback involved. Many executives pointed to the **demand for a quick payback** and ever-shorter horizons in terms of business planning.

> You need to show a fast return for any major investment. Any manager is going to have trouble justifying spending six figures this quarter if the return won't appear until next year, or the year after.

'Senior managers can be slow to commit to long-term projects that may outlive their tenure' explained one executive. Moreover an IT systems project can be 'a disruptive factor or distraction for a manager and his, or her department'.

That means there is a temptation to postpone projects until next quarter, or next year.

Cloud computing can help address the challenge of demonstrating short-term payback on a major long-term investment. This is a point highlighted in comments by many Finance executives.

> The 'pay as you' go model behind cloud computing means that the expenditure and the **payback can appear almost instantaneous.**

> The great thing about the 'pay as you go' model is that the costs, benefits and results are coupled, or linked together. You don't have to invest up front today and then wait to see a payback several quarters, or perhaps years, out.

> Another advantage of the 'pay as you go' model is the ability to validate the project, technology or return (as well as the costs) very quickly. For example by means of a pilot with as few as 5, 10 or 50 users. If the benefit or payback is **not materializing** as planned you should know straight away. It does not rely on a complex model with lots of scenarios and assumptions (which by the time it is finally completed may not be fully believed by anybody).

Is There Certainty Around Costs?

Many Finance executives suggested that their organizations would **pay a little more for the certainty around costs** that cloud-based IT can provide.

They would pay a premium to be able to better manage costs, to have complete certainty and to avoid surprises cost overruns. The following quote reflects this:

> Certainty regarding cost has a major appeal – I will spend more to know with confidence that I won't be confronted with surprises or overruns.

Another executive explained the same idea with numbers: 'If the internal cost of the IT project was 3% or 5% cheaper, but with a 10%

chance that there could be an overrun by anything up to 30% ... then it would could make sense to 'do it in the clouds''.

So will a company pay a little more in order to have certainty regarding costs? For many the answer appears to be 'yes'.

In the words of one manager, '**think of it as an insurance premium** – you spend a bit more to manage the risk of having to spend a lot more'.

Are There Economies of Scale?

The volume of users is an important factor in the decision to go cloud, or in-house, as indicated by the following comments:

> *Data centers are based on the principle of economies of scale. A service provider invests in the infrastructure on a large scale and then spreads the cost over a wide base of customers.*

> *However, there may be a point when the volume of usage reaches **a level where the economics switch**. For example when you reach hundreds or thousands of users it may make financial sense to take it back in-house.*

> *Infinite scalability is something that cloud services boast of. However, the issue of economies of scale may mean that you start with the cloud and graduate (to an in-house or hybrid model) when the volume grows.*

Project sponsors and sellers need to understand future demand and the economics related to usage as it grows. So a key question is whether economies of scale are involved and at what stage do they swing in favor of an in-house or hybrid solution?

How Will It Impact on the Income Statement / P&L?

All eyes are on the income statement or Profit & Loss Account – it is the primary means of **measuring corporate performance**. It can be a short-term and unforgiving measure.

CEOs, CFOs, shareholders and many others are nervously fixated on profit forecasts and results. That makes the impact on any IT decision on the income statement or P&L an important consideration.

How IT project costs are treated from the perspective of the income statement is very important, yet it may not be a straightforward matter.

Financial executives point out that from a P&L perspective there may be little difference between 'the cloud' and the traditional IT spend model. Counter-intuitively the latter may be cheaper in some cases. That is because the move to the cloud often results in **replacing CAPex with a higher level of OPex**.

Getting into more detail it was pointed out that the traditional upfront costs in terms of software and hardware generally don't hit the income statement straight away.

It is important for the sponsor and the salesperson to understand how IT costs are going to be treated by Finance. In particular, they need to know whether the IT costs will accounted for in the year they are incurred or amortized over a number of years.

The costs of software developed in-house or purchased externally **generally won't hit the P&L in any one year**. Rather they are often amortized or written off over a number of years. That is because it is seen as an investment in a business asset (the software) that will generate revenue over a longer period – perhaps four or five years.

Software development costs, for example, typically go onto the balance sheet and the software asset is written off in the form of an **annual amortization charge to the P&L**.

Another complicating factor is that there are often tax advantages in respect of R&D or software development in-house. So, the seller **needs a basic understanding of the accounting treatment of the proposed IT expenditure**.

For these reasons some Finance executives suggested that 'if you added up all the costs of doing it in-house, or the traditional way, and did a calculation that included the cost of funds to arrive at the equivalent of a yearly, or monthly, per user charge you might be surprised to find that the in-house option is quite competitive'.

Some pointed out that the 'pay as you go' model is surprisingly close to **how the income statement or P&L treats the investment in traditional IT**. However, the problem is that the in-house cost may not be expressed in this way – the approach varies a lot.

Those who suggested cloud computing might have a neutral effect on the company's income statement indicated that the balance sheet and the cash flow could benefit most from the move to the cloud.

What Is the 'Economic Tipping Point'?

An organization has a range of needs in terms of its IT systems and an economic argument to back up those needs. But what is it that determines which of those needs will actually get addressed in the short-term?

People may have been 'crying out' for a new or better system for a long time before the decision is made to implement it.

As one Finance executive suggested there is a 'tipping point' in respect of many IT investment decisions. That is the point at which **the requirement for a new technical solution becomes a compelling business need**.

> *What the organization needs and what the organization gets are not always the same thing however. This is particularly true in terms of legacy IT systems.*

The new IT solution may be technically superior to the old one, but the tendency in many organizations is to want to bleed existing assets. **Legacy investments represent barriers to IT in the clouds**, or indeed any new IT solutions.

There may be a case for saying that an old legacy system is costing the company money in terms of lost productivity, re-work, employee dissatisfaction, poor customer service and so on. However, these **opportunity costs are somewhat hidden** by comparison with the ticket price of a new system, or new subscription charges.

The switch to a new IT system also may require **admitting that some bad choices were made** in the past regarding IT. That too can represent a significant barrier to change.

In addition to these factors there may be switching costs involved. For example decommissioning of old systems, transferring data from the old to the new, the cost of re-training staff and so on.

The IT investment decision can be a difficult balancing act between sunk costs, switching costs and opportunity costs.

Putting It To Work

At what point will your customer reach the 'economic tipping point'? To find out, calculate the customer's:

- Sunk costs

- Switching costs
- Opportunity costs.

How Will It Impact on Liquidity and the Balance Sheet?

'The age of capital-intensive IT is over' said one executive. 'With the advent of the cloud we are entering the age of IT as a service, rather than IT as an asset on the balance sheet' he added.

For many executives the positive impact on the balance sheet and on the organization's liquidity is the cloud's number one selling point. It is there, rather than on the company's income statement, that the impact is primarily felt. Here are some comments that reflect this:

> Replacing fixed assets with 'pay as you go' services is a model **ideal for the post-credit crisis world**. It could free up thousands or hundreds of thousands that would otherwise be tied up in hardware and software.

> Thanks to the credit crunch liquidity is much more important today than it was five or 10 years ago. Cloud computing can have a positive impact on **working capital requirements** of the business.

> If capital was readily available the cloud might not have the same appeal. If the company had the funds in reserve so that it did not have to borrow and there were no other projects competing for those funds investing up front might actually make sense.

'Where does the box – the hardware or the software – sit?' That is an important question claimed another executive. 'Is it on your premises and on your balance sheet?' he continued.

Investing in IT systems traditionally involved funding the purchase or development of significant assets. In this way it put shareholder funds into software or hardware, or perhaps it even entailed borrowing money. Hence the importance of demonstrating a return on IT as an asset, or on the investment in IT.

Cloud computing offers the promise of IT as a service to the business, rather than an asset on the business balance sheet.

It may not increase the actual profits of the business, but it can impact on its **Return on Capital Employed (ROCE) or ROI** *and that is the ratio of most interest to shareholders.*

The issue of ROCE is examined in more detail in the next chapter.

5: Calculating the ROI of IT

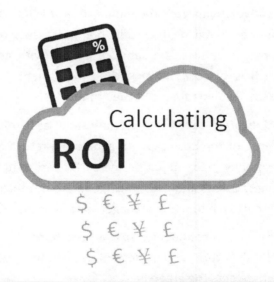

Why the Return Matters

Conversations with Finance regarding IT investment decisions inevitably end up focused on Return on Capital Employed (ROCE), or the more commonly used term Return on Investment (ROI).

ROCE 'is the primary ratio when it comes to looking at any IT spending from an investment analysis point of view'. It is a vital ingredient of 'building the economic justification required for the decision'. Here is the formula (at its simplest):

ROCE = (net operating profit / capital employed) x 100%

The ratio is important because behind every big IT decision is **a more fundamental business decision**. It is a decision about how scarce organizational resources will be leveraged to generate the maximum return. That is to say that the job of any manager is to maximize the ROCE of the business.

In the manner of a teacher about to give out homework one executive emphasized the importance of ROCE saying: 'If business A generates 5 million in profit, but has assets of 100 million, and business B returns the same profit but with assets of 50 million, then B is twice as attractive an investment as A. That is where investors would rather put their money'.

ROCE is often called the 'primary ratio' as it relates to the primary purpose of the business – to generate a return for shareholders on the money tied up in business. IT hardware and software are business assets and they must generate a return. That makes ROCE of importance to the IT managers and vendors.

Being able to confidently answer questions regarding the expected financial return could determine whether your IT project or purchase gets the green light.

Applying Investment Criteria to IT

For our friends in Finance, there were three reasons why the return on investment in respect of IT is so important:

- **Every major project or purchase must compete for funds**. For example an IT department may have an annual budget of 90 million, but projects under consideration that would require a multiple of that figure. In this era of slashed budgets, projects, departments and purchases must compete for scarce organizational resources. Money should go to those projects that promise the highest return

- **Funds cost money** – If the funds need to be borrowed then the cost is quite transparent. However, if the project is being funded out of internal reserves, retained profits or shareholder equity they are not free. The cost is in the form interest / dividend forgone. So if the real rate of return does not exceed the rate of inflation, plus the rate of commercial interest, a project or purchase will likely struggle to win support. It must generate a return higher than the cost of the funds

- **Funds will seek out the highest return** – you don't have to be Warren Buffett to know that! All other things being equal the project, purchase or initiative offering the highest rate of return is the one that should proceed. From the perspective of the Finance executive – the IT decision requires demonstrating **a compelling return on investment**. If that is not evident the funds should go elsewhere and that is something that sellers want to avoid.

The requirement to command funding is an important factor in explaining why many projects just don't get the go ahead. It applies to IT projects and purchases just as much as anything else.

ROCE in the Clouds

There are two ways in which IT projects or purchases can improve the buyer's return on investment or ROCE.

The first is by **reducing the capital that needs to be employed** within the business by:

- Freeing up, or liquidating the investment in stock, facilities, equipment, cash, etc
- Turning CAPex into OPex – for example, through a pay per use or SaaS model, or leasing rather than purchase
- Doing more for less – extending the life, or increasing the utilization of, existing assets
- Writing down the book value of assets.

The other way is to improve the return for the capital that was employed. That means impacting on the organization's top or bottom line, for example by:

- Increasing efficiency
- Reducing waste
- Cutting costs
- Reallocating costs, in particular fixed overhead
- Increasing prices or margins.

These issues relate back to the purpose of IT in the first place – its benefits and how they are measured (as discussed in earlier chapters). Finance executives pointed out these variables can be impacted on by both cloud and traditional IT models.

Because 'IT in the clouds' entails a lower upfront investment the **return is naturally going to be higher**. It should mean that you are not tying up as much cash in fixed IT investments. In theory that money should then be available to be put to other work.

The message is clear: ROCE is a major factor in the decision for or against 'IT in the clouds'. It can reduce the amount of equity or debt tied up in IT infrastructure. This sales message seems to be readily accepted among Finance executives. However there is another very important dimension of any IT investment decision – that is the impact on liquidity or cash flow.

Liquidity in the Clouds

In the post-credit crunch era, the working capital implications of any decision are an important consideration. 'IT in the clouds' can reduce the amount of money tied up long-term in IT assets on the balance sheet, but does it also have **short-term liquidity** advantages for the seller to highlight?

As one Finance executive pointed out 'business liquidity or working capital is of vital importance'. That is because 'an organization may be profitable with an impressive list of assets on its balance sheet, but if it is starved of cash it will be unable to pay its bills as they fall due'.

Liquidity becomes a key issue when bankers stop lending – as happened after the Lehmann Brothers collapse. Faced with a severe **credit crunch** CFOs had to turn elsewhere. They had to discover new sources of funding day-to-day operations, as well as strategic investment projects and programs. In such an environment 'IT in the clouds' took on new importance.

Cloud-based computing typically reduces the need to invest in business assets, such as hardware and software. But technically speaking if it is to impact on working capital it has to impact on at least one of the following four things:

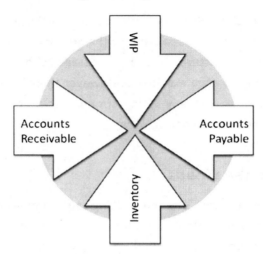

As one executive pointed out 'while it is easy to say that cloud computing frees up working capital, to justify that statement from an accounting point of view requires showing that it will impact on levels of inventory and work in progress, or accounts receivable and accounts payable'.

Most obviously a big bill to a traditional IT vendor will show up in accounts payable.

Putting It To Work

Can you summarize the relative impact on the key financial metrics for the buyer in respect of each of the key financial reports of the business – the income statement (P&L), cash flow and balance sheet?

In the table below use the two columns 'IT in the Clouds' and 'Traditional IT' to contrast the implications for both models in respect of the customer's three types of financial reports.

Impact on:	IT in the Clouds	Traditional IT
Income Statement (P&L)		
Cash Flow		
Balance Sheet		

Some Decisions Require Greater Justification

The requirement to justify IT spending is more important where spend is high and the risk is great. That brings us on to the next topic discussed in the conversations with financial executives and the second part of the IT business case equation: risk.

6: Risk 'In The Clouds'

Introduction

For IT managers this is the era of playing it safe. The appetite for risk has diminished greatly and IT managers are increasingly reluctant to put their neck on the line for a risky project, purchase or vendor. An unaddressed or unresolved risk can stall or sway the decision regarding any project or purchase.

Considerations of Risk

While purchase decisions always hold the promise of success, they also carry the risk of failure. Managers worry that the desired results will be not achieved or that other unwanted consequences will arise. This has an important bearing on their decisions.

Concerns about risk or uncertainty can make an otherwise compelling IT business case unattractive. For example although the payback from project A might be twice that of project B, the higher level of risk involved in A may make project B the winner.

The business case must include scenarios and probabilities as regards results and outcomes. It must also include a register of risk, listing each risk, rating it and outlining how it is to be managed.

Risk is a key element of the business case equation. It must be analyzed just as carefully as the numbers regarding costs, or benefits.

The Era of Playing It Safe

The extent to which IT projects and purchases are vulnerable to being stalled or swayed by risk-related concerns depends on a number of factors as listed below. Identify the ones that are relevant to your project or purchase:

- The technology involved is new
- The vendor is not well-known
- There is a lot of change and uncertainty in the air
- The business needs are unclear or corporate strategy is confused
- Technical, business and user requirements have not been clearly defined, or are subject to change
- There is poor consultation and collaboration with stakeholders and expectations are not being managed
- There is a history of previous project failures
- The buyer(s) is inexperienced or lacking in seniority
- The project does not have a powerful project sponsor
- The decision has major consequences, is high profile or big budget
- The buying decision is politically sensitive, or the number of stakeholders involved is large
- A rushed decision is being made
- There are gaps in information.

There are 13 factors listed above – that makes it an unlucky number. Count how many you have ticked in order to understand just how risky your project is. Then explore how you can help those involved to address those risks.

Preventing a Stalled Decision

Risk is often the number one reason why IT projects and purchases slow or stall. Quite naturally, when confronted with risk and uncertainty IT buyers tend to make slower and more cautious decisions. For example, the decision regarding a major IT system that once might have involved three or four steps can today involve six or eight steps and span many more months.

Risk sensitivity means IT buyers are generally advancing more cautiously towards important project or purchase decisions. In particular they are:

- Putting off making a decision as late as possible
- Leaving as many options and alternatives open as is possible
- Learning as they go, reviewing and testing options and alternatives in tandem with making a decision
- Running more pilots and proof of concepts.

When there is an underlying risk sometimes it is easier for the buyer to make no decision at all. However while all decisions entail risk, so too does a decision to do nothing.

Types of Risk

Risk, like beauty, is in the eye of the beholder. It comes in many forms, including:

- IT-related business risk
  - Has the need or strategy of the business been clearly defined?
  - Has a robust business analysis been conducted of the IT project?
  - Could a change in competition or market regulation overtake the decision?
  - Could the 'goal posts' change (a shift in corporate strategy)?
  - Will the underlying business drive for efficiency and competitiveness actually succeed?
  - Is the business actually capable of delivering on this project?
- IT project risk
  - Has the project been planned sufficiently?
  - What are the key risks, dependencies and milestones?
  - Are there any project unknowns?
  - Are there adequate controls in place?
  - Who will manage the project – do they have the experience and skill required?
  - Do we have the bandwidth to run this project successfully at this time?
  - Have we a good track record of delivering similar projects?
- IT supplier risk
  - Can the supplier deliver as promised?
  - Has the supplier a proven track record?
  - Has the supplier the resources and manpower required?
  - Can they provide solid guarantees and warrantees?
  - Will this project get their full attention?
  - Is the supplier financially solid?
- Technology risk
  - Is the technology risky? Has it been proven?
  - Will it work with our other hardware and software?
  - Is the technology future-proofed?

- o   Is it scalable? Is it secure?
- o   Is the implementation and integration likely to be smooth?
- o   Is it easy to use? Will user adoption be a challenge?
- o   What ongoing support will be needed?
- o   Are we tying ourselves into a proprietary solution / sole supplier?

- Financial risk
  - o   Is the budget robust? Is there a contingency figure?
  - o   What would be the implications of delays or overruns?
  - o   Are there any hidden costs (ongoing licenses and training)?
  - o   Has the cost / benefits analysis been validated? Do the numbers add up?
  - o   Has Finance and Procurement 'approved' the figures?
  - o   Has the budget been secured?
  - o   Are there any risks in terms of the access to, or cost of, funds?
  - o   Will the benefits materialize as planned?
  - o   Are there any other forms of exposure (currency fluctuations)?
  - o   What financial protection do we have (penalty clauses)?

- Personal – Professional risk
  - o   Could this project backfire and sabotage my career?
  - o   If I align myself too much with one stakeholder, will that hinder the project?
  - o   Am I going out on a limb with this project unless it has strong executive support?
  - o   Will working with a particular vendor or technology enhance my CV and add to my skills?

What Is the Biggest Risk?

All of the above risks should be of concern to the salesperson as they have the potential to stall or even scupper the sale. All those involved in high-stake IT decisions are in the risk management business.

Despite what you may think, the choice of supplier or technology is generally not the greatest risk in most projects. Indeed, business and project-related risks are often more important, even those they get less attention. As the list of risks shows there are a multiplicity of factors that can impinge on success.

Bringing Risk into the Open

Bringing risks and concerns out into the open is essential if they are to be addressed. However, this can be a challenge as stakeholders can be slow to admit their concerns. It also requires courage on the part of the sponsor or salesperson who may fear that bringing a risk out into the open may give it credence.

Concerns about risk can remain hidden until the point when a decision is to be made and it is too late. So some detective work may be required by the sponsor or salesperson who needs to look out for:

- An issue that raises itself repeatedly even though it was supposed to have been addressed
- There is uneasy or negative internal chatter in the corridors
- Relatively petty issues appear to take on a bigger meaning (they may be acting as a smokescreen for a hidden concern)
- A key stakeholder is quiet within the process, or appear to be withdrawn

- When requests for information or involvement by stakeholders go unanswered
- There is 'analysis paralysis' with repeated requests for more information or time to decide.

Bringing risk out into the open requires good communication and high levels of trust and needs to be done in a safe setting. Doing it in committee meetings may not be the best approach as it is easier for people to share their concerns off the record or one-to-one, such as on the fringe of a meeting (when the rest of the attendees have gone) or a more informal meeting. But the sponsor or seller has to explicitly ask the buyer about risk, albeit in a tactful and sensitive way.

Information Alleviates Risk

Risks or concerns are often the result of a lack of information or misunderstanding regarding some aspect of the IT project. Therefore identifying and plugging information gaps is the first place to start in managing risk. To minimize risk the following questions can help:

- Have we captured your requirements fully? Have we addressed the underlying businesses need?
- What do you see as the risks associated with this project? Have any risks been overlooked, underestimated or exaggerated?
- Has this been tried before? If so, was it a success? If not, what prevented it? What is different now?
- How do you think other stakeholders are feeling about the project at this time?

- Is there anybody that may be feeling uncomfortable about any aspect of the project at this stage?

- Are there any important dependencies, or contingencies that you think should be considered?

- Are there any key success factors that need to be addressed?

- Are there any areas that you would like to discuss or explore further?

- Is there anywhere that you feel additional information would be helpful?

Another Way of Discussing Risk

Some people have a concern about using the term 'risk' with their customers. They fear that it may heighten buyer anxiety and could stall the deal. That is not a problem – there is another term that is almost equally as powerful. It is 'key success factor(s)'.

Asking about the key success factors for a project or purchase is important. Even if you ask about risk it is good to invert the question in this way.

Creating a list of the key success factors gets people thinking about success and all those factors that contribute to it. It is surprising how often it throws up things that might otherwise have been overlooked.

When it comes to exploring key success factors it is helpful to categorize them as hard and soft, internal and external:

- **The 'hard' factors** include finance, people and other resources. They also include factors such as choosing the right product and supplier, getting the requirements defined adequately, or testing and implementation

- **'Soft' factors** include the attitudes and commitment of the various stakeholders, willingness of people to change old ways of working and so on
- **External factors** can include events happening in the company's industry and markets, including for example market growth rates and trends in the technology sector.

Risk 'In the Clouds'

Are IT projects 'in the clouds' more or less risky than traditional IT projects? That is a question we posed to our panel of financial executives.

For several of the Finance executives, cloud computing's greatest achievement has been the reduction of risk in the buying decision. For example, allowing users to sample the complete solution with minimal commitment, providing transparency and so on.

Risk is a key factor in the decision between cloud-based and traditional IT. It was made clear that big savings quickly lost their appeal if accompanied by a high level of risk.

As was clear from the discussions the issue of 'risk in the clouds' is multi-faceted. It is not just technology or security risk, but includes project risk, supplier risk, business and other risks – as examined below.

Project Risk

In some organizations IT has a damaged reputation regarding budgeting and cost control in respect of new projects. This project risk – the ability to deliver IT on time and to budget with the required support to the user – arose as an important factor in the decision. This is captured in the following comments:

> The statistics claiming that most IT projects are either **behind time, over budget** or in another way struggling is one of the key selling points for cloud-based services.

> Most people have had experience of an IT project or initiative that resulted in disappointment, frustration, or perhaps even worse.

The Standish Group has been tracking project success in IT for more than a decade. Their research shows that only 32% of projects succeed. It might just be one of the most powerful reasons for 'IT in the clouds' over traditional IT.

Here is what happens to the rest of the projects:

- 24% fail – they were scrapped, or simply fizzled out
- 44% were "challenged" – they ended up behind time, over budget, or failed to deliver as expected.

The Standish research highlights the specific risks to project success. It suggests that nearly 50% of success can be attributed as follows:

- Executive support (18%)
- User involvement (16%)
- The project manager's experience (14%).

Some of the other reasons why projects succeed (rather than fail) include:

- Clear objectives (12%)
- Minimized scope (10%)
- Firm requirements (6%).

These numbers take the mystery out of why so many IT projects fail.

> Organizations with a **low level of IT confidence or capability** are likely to migrate fastest to the cloud. Those with a poor track record

in terms of delivering IT projects on time and within budget, and a bad reputation in terms of satisfying internal stakeholders and supporting end users are most under threat from migration to the cloud.

Some Finance executives suggested that cloud-based software services could have the advantage of facilitating **increased user adoption** – a problem that often dogs new IT systems. Because they were based on a subscriber model, issues of ease of use, as well as help and support, tend to be well addressed.

You could argue that cloud services are much less concerned with technology and more focused on the end user, the outcome and the service expectation. Plus they are designed to be used 'right out of the box'.

Others suggested that because cloud-based services tended to be designed for the masses the extent of **customization** possible might be limited. In certain situations that could swing the decision back in favor of traditional in-house hosted solutions.

Technical Risk

Although the audience was not technical, the issue of technical risk arose. In particular, several had experiences of IT projects or systems that had run into problems.

For many of the executives these risks were greatly reduced, if not eliminated, by cloud computing. The following comment is typical of this view:

*Typically IT in the cloud involves a very different buying process. It is **much easier to try it out** – to sample with minimal commitment.*

Can Google, Amazon and Microsoft run a data warehouse or server farm cheaper than us? One that is more cost-effective, robust, scalable and greener too? Probably! After all that is what they specialize in.

Service providers have economies of scale, innovative technologies, advanced management systems and lots more besides. That is their business – our business is electronics assembly not web farm management!

*Naturally I would expect them to have a **technology, cost and efficiency advantage** over us. Whether it is '4 nines reliability' or anything else they are likely to have the edge.*

On the other side of 'the technical debate' **integration was raised as a risk**. In particular, the ability to migrate data to the cloud and integrate with other systems (ranging from ERP or legacy databases) was highlighted. In this context it would appear that some of those interviewed doubted the cloud's sweeping inter-operability claims.

Security Risk

The issue of security tends to steal the headlines in respect of cloud computing, however financial executives did not appear to get too worked up about it. They seemed to adopt what might be described as 'a balanced view' of the issue.

*Are we going to put **mission critical systems** on a public cloud, or highly sensitive corporate data for that matter? The answer is 'no'. There are many steps to be taken on the pathway to the full adoption of cloud computing before either of these decisions would be taken. Also it is not an 'either / or' decision, because there are hybrid models, such as the private cloud, to be considered.*

One executive said he had read an article on cloud computing recently which basically said 'the cloud was safer'. It argued that 'corporations were focused on perimeter defense, while cloud services were secure all the way through using https and had no single point of failure'. In the words of the executive such sweeping claims are not credible – you have to **address the security issue on a case-by-case basis'.**

There are probably as many levels of security in the cloud as in the corporate environment. The security question depends on how good your corporate security is, as well as the level of security you need.

The advice was to find out what the security requirements are for each business and for each application.

Supplier Risk

The choice of supplier is obviously a key factor in the cloud computing decision.

Supplier-related risks were highlighted by some of the executives, including the **risk of a supplier going out of business,** failing to deliver the service levels required, or to protect the data.

Obviously there is a comfort in dealing with the big players, such as Microsoft Azure, Google, or Amazon Web Services. With smaller players extra care is required.

'It is a little like as if you were investing in one of those SaaS companies' said one executive. 'You have to **choose the right partner'** he added, 'treat it like an investment decision'. The recommendation from another executive was to do 'a due diligence on the supplier in question', including:

- How financially secure is the supplier?
- Is it fully compliant with best practice in all areas from compliance to security?
- What is the SLA and what are the commitments of the supplier where service levels fall short?
- Does the company serve others in our industry?

- Where are the data centers located?
- What jurisdiction does the business operate in?
- Other factors, such as ownership, structure and growth objectives of the company.

Financial Risk

Not surprisingly, given the background of those being interviewed, financial risk arose for discussion. It encompassed a number of areas, including:

- Issues associated with adding to the debt of the company in order to pay for a major IT investment in the traditional manner. This includes the risk of a rise in interest rates, as well as the impact on the balance sheet of the business
- The risk that the project would not generate the financial return required to justify the investment, otherwise referred to as 'business risk'. This could happen either because costs exceeded what was anticipated or because the savings or additional revenue fell short of what was expected.

For the reasons outlined in **Chapter 3** the level of **financial risk associated with IT in the clouds** was generally perceived to be lower than traditional IT. The reasons included:

- Greater certainty around costs
- Smaller upfront investment
- Funds do not need to be borrowed
- Move visible / lower total cost of ownership.

Putting It To Work

So, risk is an important factor in the IT buying decision and, as the following table suggests, is an important means of comparing traditional IT with IT in the clouds.

	IT in the Clouds	Traditional IT
Project Risk		
Technical Risk		
Supplier Risk		
Business Risk		
Financial Risk		
Security Risk		
Compliance Risk		
Other Risks		

To use this table, complete each column marking the two alternatives as on a scale from very low to very high in terms of risk.

An informed discussion about risk is a key part of the IT investment decision. The advice for vendors is to **bring risk out into the open** and to address it head on.

Here is an example of a risk management table. Can you document the risks to your project's success in the format overleaf?

Risk Management Table Example

	Risk A	Risk B	Risk C
Risk	Supplier fails		
Probability	3%		
Worst Case Outcome	Extra Cost: 125k; Lost Earnings: 100k; No support; No upgrades; System falls over; Lost operating days /revenue; Must retain new vendor; Extra development effort.		
Managed Outcome	Extra Cost:25k; Lost Earnings: 0K; Managed exit of supplier; Handover to another supplier & internal resources; Managed transition – no downtime.		
Strategies for Risk Mitigation	Financial due diligence before selection of supplier; Engage our system integration partner; Get our own people trained up; Ensure it is fully documented; Access to source code; Bond from vendor; Software in escrow; Software acceptance testing / handover; License fee & terms to allow for contingency; Integration partner to manage delivery.		

	Risk A	Risk B	Risk C
Monitoring and Contingency	Make supplier resilience part of quarterly project review process; Five-step plan ready to be activated if required (last updated Nov 2013).		
Risk Owner	CTO		

7: Compliance 'In The Clouds'

Introduction

Mounting compliance requirements are an increasingly important factor in IT investment decisions.

Whether it is adherence to internal standards or external regulations, compliance is now a key element of the IT business case.

The Growing Compliance Agenda

The IT compliance agenda is broader than at first it would appear.

At its simplest the role of IT compliance centers on preventing penalties and fines, as well as the adverse publicity, associated with non-compliance in respect of **laws, regulations, rules and standards**.

However compliance means different things to different people as the countless IT business cases developed using our tools suggest.

Compliance is a term that encompasses **a wide range of objectives**. Here are the 12 most common ones:

- Guard the company's **data** (and the customer's data too)

- Prevent disclosure of **organizational secrets**
- Reduce the risk of **fraud**
- Ensure business **resilience** in the face of any potential IT disaster
- Improve data **accuracy** and reporting throughout the business
- Ensure that **IT is used optimally within the business** and delivers the promised organizational efficiency and other benefits
- Protect and ensure proper use of organizational IT **assets**
- Guide and manage the **conduct of employees** in respect of how IT is used
- Manage **performance / service levels** (SLA compliance) for end users from both internally and externally provided applications, or services
- Manage **IT inventory** and control spend (including software license reconciliation)
- Ensure **corporate wide technical uniformity** and interoperability in respect of IT systems
- Managing the **green agenda** and other aspects of the corporate social policy.

It is clear that IT compliance has many dimensions and that its importance goes far beyond the IT department. That makes the above list of 12 compliance drivers a useful checklist.

Given the breadth of the topic of compliance it is important to **clarify what compliance means** to any particular customer and indeed for each particular stakeholder.

Compliance in the Clouds

We asked financial executives about IT compliance in the age of the cloud – that is the implications for compliance with not just laws and regulations, but also with:

- Internal governance policies
- Codes of practice
- Industry standards
- Standard operating procedures
- In-house guidelines / established norms
- Contracts, including SLAs
- Industry best practices.

The executives much preferred talking about numbers than they did about compliance (and indeed anything else!) However, when the conversation got going it quickly became clear that Finance executives had a **zero-risk approach to compliance** in respect of IT, as well as other areas.

There was a 'take no chances' mind-set, particularly among those in large organizations. To the surprise of the Finance executive, this cautious view was not necessarily held by other managers.

Un-official Computing in the Clouds

Many of the executives talked about a **creeping unofficial usage of cloud-based applications**. It often started with people using apps on their iPads, or with applications such as Dropbox and Skype. The next step was for managers to start using SaaS solutions in respect of marketing, human resource development (HRD), learning and development and so on.

Executives suggested that some managers embraced applications based in the clouds as a means of avoiding IT, fast-tracking a project, or side-stepping a drawn-out investment appraisal decision.

However, the view was that a **'free-for-all'**, where managers and employees could choose their own 'pet' applications, was to be avoided. As one executive put it: 'at the end of the day somebody has to have control over the company's data, its network and its technology'.

GRC in the Clouds

Several of the executives grouped compliance under the GRC banner, addressing the issues of **Governance, Risk and Compliance** in tandem.

Given the importance of IT to the business it was seen as a key element of good corporate governance overall. In addition, IT plays a role in compliance and governance in many non-IT functions of the business.

Of prime importance to Finance was the role of IT in the organization-wide information gathering and reporting, as well as in terms of financial information.

Some executives saw IT in the role of **guardians of corporate data** – a role that was particularly important in the context of cloud computing.

Compliance Implications of the Cloud

Does computing in the clouds make the company more vulnerable in terms of security, compliance, and risk management?

This was something that the Finance executives struggled to answer. Several suggested that the question was abstract and that the answer was 'it depends'.

Some systems and data were more important than others, in terms of the extent to which they exposed the organization to compliance, financial and other threats. So the view was that the compliance issue needed to be considered on a **case by case basis**.

The Compliance Burden

While the tendency was to 'err on the side of caution' when it comes to compliance, it was recognized that compliance adds significant business complexity and cost.

'Over-compliance' as one executive described it, in terms of applying security or redundancy to basic non-strategic IT applications, should be avoided.

Compliance with relevant laws and regulations often comes with a **heavy administrative burden** as compliance must be audited regularly. Would computing in the clouds impact on this, either positively or negatively? This was something that the Finance executives struggled to answer.

One executive suggested it might help in respect of some applications. That is because hosted solutions tend to facilitate monitoring of levels of service, usage, and performance and to provide quite detailed reporting capabilities.

Another executive pointed out that cloud-based computing should simplify the aspect of compliance concerned with license management. Auditing software and hardware licenses, tracking usage and identifying unused assets is an important activity and traditionally can be demanding on resources.

Several pointed out that compliance management was not something that could be delegated to third parties – it was simply too important. So even if managers were provided with greater visibility in terms of more detailed reports or automated alerts, the responsibility for compliance still remained with them.

The point was made that the organization needs to plan ahead of time for **future compliance requirements**. Managers should be concerned not just with today's standards and regulations, but those of tomorrow too.

Whose Regulations Apply?

The lack of a coherent set of international standards governing 'IT in the clouds' was highlighted by one of the executives.

'Which compliance regime will apply?' That becomes an important issue if the cloud-based service provider has **centers in multiple countries, all with different national regulations**.

A key area raised was data privacy and protection in terms of regulatory requirements, as well as data security from the perspective of protecting against competitive espionage.

However, in considering the legislative environment, other factors included commercial law, taxation law and intellectual property rights.

You may want the data hosted in your local market, or a market where the regulatory regime is considered most ideal. So, where the provider is located could be a factor in what supplier is chosen.

What Does the SLA Say?

When it came to IT compliance in the clouds, several executives stressed the importance of the reputation and strength of the service provider.

Others pointed out the **importance of studying the Service Level Agreement** (SLA) or contract terms of the provider. This is a key document in terms of addressing the issue of compliance of a hosted service.

If the provider is big and you are small then you have little choice but to take or leave what is in the supplier's standard SLA. But of course, if you are big enough then you can probably dictate the standards, the service levels and what goes into the SLA.

Use the following as a checklist, identifying the specific compliance requirement and the owner(s) or relevant manager:

- Laws and regulations
- Internal governance policies
- Industry standards
- Codes of practice
- Standard operating procedures
- In-house guidelines / established norms
- Contracts, including SLAs
- Industry best practices.

For any relevant compliance requirement describe the risk of non-compliance and the associated compliance burden for your customer. Then outline the impact of your solution.

8: Strategy 'In The Clouds'

Introduction

Today's IT decisions are more strategic than ever before. As managers put it, IT projects and purchases must fit with the longer-term IT strategy, as well as with the broader business goals and strategies of the organization. That is why the term 'strategic fit' is an important element of the business case.

Managers must demonstrate that the IT project or purchase fits with the pre-existing jigsaw of priorities, goals and strategies – not just within IT but organization-wide.

Today's IT buying decisions are not just a matter of technology. They are first and foremost business decisions. They revolve around the needs of the business and what it is trying to achieve.

What Is a Strategic IT Project?

To be successful an IT project or purchase must be seen to be 'strategic'. But what does strategic mean? Well, there are different interpretations, but we see seven elements in those IT projects considered to be most strategic. You can use this list to see just how strategic is your IT project.

'Strategic' means:

- **Connecting with the strategy** of the business, as well as the overall IT strategy of the organization. It means connecting with what the business is trying to achieve. The importance of any IT project or purchase derives from the strategy that it supports. The manager who wants to fast-track any project or purchase must piggy-back on an important strategy within the business – whether it is a strategy for new product innovation, increased business efficiency, or cost reduction

- **Focusing on results and performance**. Indeed there is nothing more strategic than results. That means project sponsors must demonstrate the purchase will help the organization (or part thereof) to achieve its objectives and boost its performance. The link between spending on technology and achieving business results must be clear

- **Reflecting priorities** – it is about what is important. With a diverse portfolio of projects and purchases competing for scarce organizational resources, managers must be able to demonstrate that their purchase or project is more relevant and compelling than others. The sponsor and seller must show that a particular IT project or purchase is a priority if it is to be funded and funded now. The temptation in any organization is to put projects that are not a priority 'onto the long finger'

- **Seeing the bigger picture**. So the project or purchase must be shown to fit with past decisions, or investments, as well as future ones – that is the IT roadmap of the organization as well as its present and future competitive strategy.

- **Timing**. The sponsor and seller must show that the timing is right for the investment and that there is a penalty involved in delaying a decision. It must be sensitive to everything else

that is happening in the organization at the time. A good
project presented at the wrong time will struggle. Getting the
timing right is key and the successful sponsor knows when to
put his or her project or idea forward

- **Taking the longer-term view**. It involves setting a course into
the future, one that avoids zigzag courses of action. For
example there is no point in IT exploring new back office
administration system upgrades, when another team is
advanced in the process of exploring out-sourcing options.
Any IT investment must be shown to be future-proofed and
capable of delivering over into the long term. At the same
time managers face the challenge of showing an immediate
payback – either this quarter or the next

- **Taking an integrated view.** Too often we hear the comment
'that team is off doing their own thing ...' The result is an
uncoordinated approach doomed to mediocrity by limited
stakeholder involvement and poor buy-in. Any IT decision has
to be shown to make sense not just within the context of the
overall IT budget / strategy, but within the context of the
overall business. It has to demonstrate 'joined-up thinking'.

So, just how strategic is your project, or purchase? To find out count
how many of the seven factors listed above apply. To become more
strategic work on the factors that are not present.

How to Make Any IT Project More Strategic

The challenge for IT project sponsors and managers is to **connect
their project with the results** that the business is trying to achieve –
to connect with what managers care about most – the strategy,

performance and results of their business, project, department or team.

If the project or purchase is not, of itself, strategically important, then the sponsor / seller must **find out what is and connect with it**. If it does not contribute directly to corporate strategy and the P&L the CEO or CFO may know, or care, little about it. However, that does not mean it is not important in other ways. For example to:

- Specific stakeholders, or departments
- Particular projects, facilities, or functions
- The achievement of particular milestones, metrics, or other results
- The buyer with a specific challenge at that point in time.

Making **tangible the link** between your project and the success of the relevant stakeholders is key. With this in mind, select a key customer and identify what matters to them – identify their definition of success, strategy for success, key success factors, metrics for success, and risks or barriers to success.

Business Results Are the Route to Being Strategic

The shift in the balance of power in terms of buying and budget decisions has implications for which IT projects or purchases succeed.

Specifically the role of Procurement, Finance and others in IT decisions means that sponsors must engage with the business and economic buyer, communicating why you matter in a language that they understand. Increasingly that is the language of numbers and the business case (or economic justification for the purchase).

The imagination of business buyers – especially those from Procurement and Finance – is not going to be captured by the traditional technology features and benefits message.

They want something they can put in a spreadsheet and see translated into future revenue, profit or asset value projections. They will sit up and pay attention to project sponsors and managers who quantify results and communicate a compelling business case.

The implication is that IT project sponsors and managers need to stop explaining why their project or technology is so great and instead communicate how the business will be better as a result. Those results are the route to an IT project or purchase being seen as strategic.

The Future of Computing

There appears to be agreement among Finance executives that cloud computing marks 'a significant step in **the evolution of corporate computing**'. Most appeared to agree that it represents the future of computing, yet they were cautious about predicting the rapid move of all corporate computing to the cloud.

In the words of many 'it is early days yet' and how the industry will evolve is 'difficult to predict'. Several expressed discomfort about the level of hype regarding computing in the clouds, with the comment being made that vendor hype sometimes confused the issue for many companies.

> The issue at hand is how we get from where we are today in terms of **past IT investments and legacy systems** to the idealized cloud computing environment and that includes issues of security, standards and compliance.

How this fits in with the broader objectives of the business and the longer term strategy for IT as well as the end user or business function (sales or support in respect of CRM) is key. The decision cannot be made in isolation of the bigger picture.

A Strategic View of IT in the Clouds

Is the decision to embrace 'computing in the cloud' a strategic one? The answer for most of the executives was 'yes'. For most IT was, or at least should be, 'strategic'.

Here are eight reasons why IT was considered strategic:

- **Significant amounts have been invested in IT** within many organizations. That means bleeding these assets is important. IT also means that you are not starting from a greenfield situation, but rather what may be 'a mish-mash' of existing systems. So any IT decision must take place within this context

- What you commit to today has **long-term implications** and changing later on is likely to be costly. Decisions should be taken slowly and carefully, with zigzag courses of action being avoided

- You cannot have different parts of the business adopting their own systems or standards. A **uniformed approach and consistent standards** are required so that the different systems can talk to each other and security and other policies are adhered to

- The approach to planning IT has to be integrated with **what the business is trying to achieve.** IT's role is a strategic one – it is to improve the competitiveness and efficiency of an organization. It is only a means to an end, rather than an end in itself

- There is an **IT element to most strategies** within the business, whether the strategy concerns production efficiency, HR, supply chain management, or sales. IT has to be part of the strategic planning process in so many areas of the business

- The level of **dependence on IT** has reached such a level that it moves the issue of business resilience up the agenda. There are real IT-related threats in respect of data security, disaster recovery or compliance

- IT is about **future-proofing the business** – in areas ranging from mobile access to data and applications by the workforce, to BIG DATA. In this respect IT should be proactive, rather than reactive in terms of how it is planned

- Important IT projects often **involve considerable change within the organization** – changes that impact on people, processes and many other areas. They need executive sponsorship at the highest levels and ensuring end user adoption is a key success factor.

The factors listed above, in addition to underpinning the strategic importance of most IT-related decisions, point to the need for slower and more cautious decision-making. Understandably the need for caution is greatest when something is new or untried.

There is clearly **a strategic dimension to how managers think about IT**. For this reason some might argue that this perspective is more characteristic of the traditional IT decision involving high risk and major upfront costs.

Regardless, the eight points listed above are a useful checklist in terms of the potential 'strategic impediments' to the adoption of 'IT in the cloud'. They are also a guide for project sponsors and sellers who want to communicate the reasons why their project matters.

Innovation in the Clouds

What about **innovation as a strategy**? Perhaps in keeping with the stereotype of the Finance executive there was a circumspect view of technical innovation. There can be disadvantages to being a first mover, which was reflected by comments such as:

> You don't necessarily want to be an early adopter of any new technology fad – you would rather that other people try it first and let them iron 'out the kinks'.

Many executives displayed a split personality regarding IT and innovation. While they talked about the risks associated with innovation, they also believed that 'you don't want to fall behind ...'. Clearly getting the balance right is important.

The **technological sophistication of your industry** (or your customer's industry) is a key factor in determining the pace of adoption for any new innovation. For example your customers and supply chain partners may expect to be able to interact with your business through user-friendly cloud based applications.

There was an interesting point made by one executive: it is the data (and what is done with it) rather than the application that is the core business asset. New cloud-based applications that enable an organization to better **access and leverage its existing data** can have a powerful appeal. Whether that is enabling mobile access to corporate systems and data, or something else, the key is that these are not competing with a capability or a system that the company already has.

The IT Department in the Clouds

The question arose as to '**what aspects of IT are strategic and are not strategic?**' This was suggested as an important consideration in the cloud debate. In particular, those services that were less strategic might be more readily migrated to the cloud.

Some Finance executives suggested that it was inevitable that IT would follow a trend evident in many other areas of the business – that is out-sourcing.

After all, '**why not outsource IT too?**' This would then allow the organization to 'focus more on its core business – whether than is pharmaceuticals, or professional services'.

Few organizations see developing software or running data warehouses as a core competence or competitive advantage for their business. So, outsourcing these activities 'is not like cutting off an arm, or a leg'. The business can thrive without doing them in-house.

In many cases the conversation about strategy quickly led into a debate about the structure of IT, or what **the IT department of the future** of would look like. Therefore, as we will see in the next chapter, there is a political dimension to IT computing in cloud.

Putting It To Work

- List three **business initiatives, projects or strategies** that your IT product / solution impacts upon?

- What is the **vision for the future** of the customer's IT department in the clouds, or based on traditional IT? (skills level, employees, projects, budget, etc.)

9: Politics 'In The Clouds'

Introduction

Just as in any other area of corporate decision-making there is an element of politics involved in many IT decisions. That is why it is added as the final element of the business case equation.

There is politics involved in IT decisions, just as there is in any other area. With multiple projects competing for the same limited pool of resources there will inevitably be winners and losers in terms of project sponsors and stakeholders.

Seducing Stakeholders

Aligning stakeholders is one of the key challenges faced by IT project sponsors and managers. Given the multiplicity of stakeholders involved it often requires reconciling divergent needs and requirements. It is an issue that runs over the full lifecycle of the project, for example:

- Garnering support to get the project off the ground
- Eliciting stakeholder requirements
- Communicating project progress

- Training and supporting users in the adoption of any new technologies.

For many managers there is a growing realization that technology is only a part of the IT equation. As one manager put it: 'IT decisions within large organizations are as much about people and their problems, as they are about hardware or software'.

That makes the choice of project manager crucially important. More specifically people and political skills are a key ingredient of the effective project manager:

> *A software genius who prefers working at a keyboard than engaging with people is going to struggle to engage with the various stakeholders, or to communicate in their language. That can be a major handicap for the project.*

The term 'seducing stakeholders' describes the requirement of a successful IT project. Some of the inherent stakeholder challenges facing the sponsor are to:

- Overcome stakeholder inertia
- Fend off competition from other projects
- Engage stakeholders and building commitment
- Manage shareholder expectations
- Assuage genuine fears and concerns
- Manage hidden agendas and politics.

People Equals Politics

Modern buying requires more committees and consensus. Indeed, the buyers and sellers we talked to suggest that the numbers involved in major buying decisions has doubled in a decade. Multifunctional buying teams are the order of the day, together with a high level of consultation and involvement for all stakeholders.

Of course more people involved in the process means more politics and requires reconciling a greater diversity of personalities and viewpoints. This elongates buying cycles and from the seller's point of view increases the degree of uncertainty involved.

Competing for Limited Resources

An IT department is likely to have many competing, and perhaps even conflicting, projects. Those projects are all 'going to the same well' looking for funding. However, there is not enough money to go around and that means priorities must be set and compromises need to be made.

The issue is not just about access to funds; there are other resource implications too. There is only sufficient bandwidth within the IT department (and indeed the organization) to progress so many projects successfully simultaneously.

Every project requires a certain amount of management attention, an appropriately skilled and experienced project manager and it also may require software engineers and developers. All these resources are limited.

In an ideal world IT projects and purchases compete on their merits – that is on an objective analysis of the costs and benefits. In a 'Darwinian' manner projects should compete for resources and only the best should survive. However, projects don't just compete on economics, but on a political basis too.

Sponsors and stakeholders have a vested interest in certain projects. They want their projects to progress and to proceed, ahead of others. In this end they will make their case in whatever way they can. That includes using strategies that come under the heading of 'how to win friends and influence people'.

What Makes Decisions Political?

Here are some of the characteristics of IT decisions that are highly political:

- There are big egos or personalities involved
- Somebody risks losing face, or losing power or resources
- There are many projects competing for a shrinking budget
- People's jobs or promotions are on the line
- Old ways of doing things are being questioned, undermined, or threatened
- There is an element of vanity associated with the project
- There are many stakeholders with divergent interests
- There have been past negative experiences – leading to caution and trepidation
- There is a culture of political favoritism, canvassing and cronyism in the organization
- Some stakeholders are attempting to justify past decisions
- The team involved is newly formed and yet to develop an effective way of working together collaboratively
- There is a high degree of risk and uncertainty involved
- There is a competitive rather than a co-operative culture within the organization
- There is a culture of blame or fear, poor leadership and a low trust environment

- The budgeting process, basis for evaluating key projects and allocating resources or decision-making process is weak and lacks transparency.

The project promoter and the salesperson must look out for all of the above factors as they make the success of even a compelling business case uncertain.

In this context the successful business case will involve a process of extensive involvement with stakeholders and will be written, or at least reviewed, by a cross-functional committee. This is essential to creating the buy-in required to get the project sanctioned as well as to ensure successful implemented. Seducing stakeholders is a key requirement.

Put It To Work: What Stakeholders Do You Matter To?

List the various stakeholders involved in the buying decision for your solution. Then for each identify what matters to them and how your product or service (either directly or indirectly) impacts on it. Don't forget to include all the relevant business functions, including for example Procurement, Finance and Operations, as well as the end user.

Stakeholders	What matters to these stakeholders	How we can impact on what matters to them
Operations Manager	*Time required to set up a new production run*	*Our equipment is designed for rapid switch over, the process of set up can begin while the machine is still in operation*

You might like to approach this same challenge another way. Use the table below to list the key benefits or features of your product (column 1). Then in the second column identify how each feature or benefit impacts on the customer's performance and success. In the final column identify the stakeholder for whom the feature / benefit matters.

Key Feature / Benefit of Your Solution	How It Impacts on Performance / Success	The Stakeholder(s) for whom IT Matters
Detailed user logs and reporting	*Enables full traceability and simplifies reporting*	*Compliance and Quality Control*

Based on the above analysis are there any stakeholders that you have been neglecting in terms of:

- Communicating the results you can help them achieve?
- Contributing to their success?

Focus on how you can contribute more to their success, for example by:

- Providing insights and information that they don't have, challenging old ways of thinking and providing a new perspective
- Helping them to solve their problems (or at least to see their problems in new ways)
- Removing obstacles and barriers to success

- Tackling opportunities and challenges
- Overcoming fears, helping them to look to the future, to transition or change
- Helping them to become more competitive, dynamic and efficient
- Offering new ideas and creativity in facing old problems
- Reducing their level of risk, uncertainty or exposure.

The Buying Decision Can Be Messy

To the salesperson the buying decision is relatively straightforward, particularly for those with a strong belief in their product / solution. For the buyer the 'straightforward solution' may suggest that the salesperson does not fully understand their needs.

Similarly buyers often cast a jaundiced eye over the analyst's statistics, magic quadrants, and best practice guides waved before them by vendors. As one buyer said to us recently 'there is the ideal world and the real world and the two are quite different places'.

He continued 'buying in large organizations requires reconciling contradictory and sometimes conflicting demands, it cannot be divorced from past decisions, or present day politics, or personalities ... increasingly it requires making the best of what you have got, rather than starting with a clean sheet, or a greenfield'.

The buyer's real requirements are often messy and sometimes contradictory. There is a maze of internal, as well as the external, drivers, both spoken and unspoken, that shape the purchase agenda. These include:

- Competing projects and alternatives
- Complicating factors

- Trade-offs and compromises
- Hidden agendas
- Sometimes-conflicting motivations, including politics and culture.

Buying decisions are often bound up with trade-offs, compromises and politics that the salesperson typically does not see. The buying case is a logical-analytical framework for decision-making. However because buyers are not computers, impulse and emotion inevitably impact on the decision too.

Political Implications for the IT Department

Another aspect of the IT decision is the political implications of a move to the cloud. In particular the decision for or against the cloud may have implications for the future of the IT Department.

Cloud computing was recognized as both presenting opportunities and threats to existing IT departments. Some argued that it could eventually lead to a **loss of budget, headcount and indeed power** for many IT departments. That means it 'won't happen overnight' they claimed. However, this view was not held by all.

Predicting the Future

Predicting the future is something that many of the executives are cautious about. The rapid pace of technology change is something that makes forecasting the future of IT particularly risky.

*You have to be careful in **forecasting technology trends**. Think of the mobile phone, social media and even e-readers. Who could have predicted how quickly they would become a feature of everyday life?*

Will cloud computing have the same impact as the Internet, or digital media for example? Well probably! But who can really predict what will happen.

In the early stages of any new technology it can be hard for the reality to **'live up to all the hype'**. The pace of adoption can be slower than the press releases and vendor marketing suggest. That said, it can obviously end up changing entirely how we see IT.

The famous Arthur C Clarke quote (paraphrased below) echoed in some of the discussions regarding just how much cloud computing would change IT:

We overestimate technology in the short-term, but we underestimate it in the long-term.

The IT Department of the Future

'I have no doubt that the IT department of tomorrow will be **radically different from today'** – this statement was echoed by many of the executives. It is evident from the following comments:

I can see IT becoming the broker of a range of services to its internal customers with a growing proportion being provisioned via the cloud.

The function will increasingly involve matching internal customers and their requirements with external services. The question is not 'if?' but 'when?' this will happen.

*A **different kind of IT person** will be required in the future – not the guy who can take the back off a machine or write a batch of code. The person will be more like a business analyst, adept at matching business needs with technology solutions and focused on getting the most out of IT solutions available in the marketplace, rather than creating their own.*

Some executives talked about what had previously been technological challenges, in areas such as marketing, sales and services, being somewhat divorced from the underlying technology and perhaps even IT.

Availing from a range of SaaS solutions that are essentially 'plug and play' in nature could **shift the focus from technical challenges to business solutions**. For example, how the business benefits will be realized and user adoption ensured. This could be a double-edged sword for IT – having potential advantages and disadvantages.

On the one hand it meant a new **'more strategic interface between IT and the business user'**. This is something that may please many IT directors.

There are some stakeholder groups that can be more difficult for IT to deal with, perhaps because they are overly demanding, have a limited grasp of technology and unclear or conflicting requirements. Dealing with these groups may be easier with respect to the implementation of cloud-based IT services.

For example it is easier to implement a CRM system that has been proven and has 40 million users, than to try and get stakeholders together to agree on building your own.

Rather than getting bogged down in 'domain' areas such as the functionality of the payroll system, or the features of a marketing platform, **IT could focus in on core technology issues**, or project management of the successful implementation.

When it comes to marketing or HR software – the software code becomes less important – how it is written, or what it is written in is probably no longer a key success factor. So, attention turns to what the software is going to help the business to achieve – to the functionality as required by marketing, HR or the other business user.

*Attention turns from **how it works to the benefits it delivers** – that is probably where it should always have been.*

On the other hand the availability of 'neatly packaged out-of-the-box' cloud-based IT solutions, others felt might lead to a marginalization of the role of IT. As one executive pointed out 'it means that managers and their departments are **no longer wholly dependent on the IT department** and what it can deliver. They can avail of the best of what the IT industry world-wide can deliver ...'.

The Political Implications for IT

Opinions were divided as to whether cloud computing would politically be advantageous or disadvantageous for the IT department within large organizations.

However, there was agreement that regardless of what happens IT will still have an important role to play in how the organization uses technology – that is regardless of the proportion of applications or data hosted in the clouds *versus* internally.

Part 2

Building the Business Case

10: Selling to Logical-Analytical Buyers

Introduction

There is an erroneous assumption about how buyers buy that is surprisingly common in selling. It is a major impediment to success for IT salespeople who hold it. Yet they seem blissfully unaware of their error.

How you sell is based on assumptions about the type of buyer you are selling to and more specifically about how those buyers make their purchase decisions.

The consequences of getting it wrong are a mismatch between buyer and seller and ultimately a lost sale.

An Erroneous Sales Assumption

To find out if you are in danger of misreading the modern IT buyer, or the buying decision, take the following test.

Of the following three statements – which best describes how your customers buy? Is it number 1, number 2 or number 3?

1. **Potential clients buy things** based on instinct and emotion, or based on a relationship with the salesperson. Then they justify their purchases logically

2. **Potential customers are completely hard-nosed and analytical** – there is no room for impulse or emotion in their decision-making

3. **Potential customers are rational and analytical,** but of course there can be other factors involved, such as gut instinct, buyer prejudices and personal motivations.

The answer you picked reveals as much about your sales approach as it does about the true nature of how your customers buy. That is because the assumptions you make about how your customers buy inevitably influence the sales approach you adopt.

If you assume that customers decide first and rationalize later then your approach will be different to the salesperson who sees his buyers as numbers-obsessed and analytical.

The question is whether you adapt your sales approach based on how logical / emotional each buyer is? Getting it wrong can result in a costly misalignment between buyer and seller.

The Three Types of Buyers

The above test is based on a simple yet powerful concept. There are three types of buyers, as follows:

- Totally Instinctive / Emotional
- Strictly Rational
- Balanced or Normal (falling in the middle, between the first two).

Because there are three types of buyers there really needs to be three types of selling – one for each type of buyer.

The Correct Answer to the Test

So what was your answer – 1, 2, or 3? And is it the right answer? Well, everybody's business is different, so obviously it depends. The majority of buyers believe that they are more logical and analytical than intuitive and emotional. Also there is a concerted effort in procurement circles to make sure it is so.

Yes, buyers can instinctively decide in an instant whether they like or trust a particular salesperson and they must 'feel right' about any decision they are going to make, but there is no question that there is more rigor around buying IT. In respect of how most corporations spend their money this is the age of the economic buyer and the cost / benefits analysis.

Yet it is surprising how often we hear the answer '1' from salespeople – that is 'customers buy emotionally and justify rationally'. It is even said about buyers in large multinational organizations! The question is 'do you give the buyer enough credit for being rational and able to make the 'right decision'?'

Meet the Logical Buyer

The top eight reasons why buyers are more logical than you might think are as follows:

- **Budgets have been cut** with more purchases and projects competing for scarce resources and mounting pressure to drive down / curtail spending and reduce supplier costs
- **Procurement** is setting and policing the standards (and indeed targets) for ever more professionalized buying
- **Policies and procedures** increasingly govern how buying decisions are made – they are designed to reduce, retard and regiment spending
- Buying decisions have been wrested away from the front line and now require **sign off or approval** from senior managers
- Increasingly buying decisions are being made by **cross-functional buying teams**
- **Approved vendor and product lists**, as well as procurement systems, limit the discretion of buyers to decide
- Decisions are increasingly being **reviewed post-purchase**, with managers being held accountable for decisions made

- **A cost / benefits analysis** is increasingly required for large (as well as not so large) purchases.

These factors are causing a shift in how buying decisions are made, as shown in the diagram below.

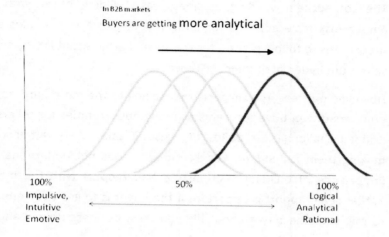

In B2B markets

Buyers are getting more analytical

100%	50%	100%
Impulsive,		Logical
Intuitive		Analytical
Emotive		Rational

The advice for sellers of IT is to expect buyers to be logical, rational and analytical.

Why Do Sellers Underestimate Buyers?

Why are we prone to underestimate just how logical the buyer really is? Well, one of the key reasons is that buying decisions are increasingly taking place behind closed doors – so sellers don't get to see the real level of complexity as a result.

Another is that sellers are unaware of the rise of Procurement's power and the wave of procurement processes, policies and systems that has ensued. Perhaps some buyers are even happy to be underestimated by sellers.

If the buyer is logical does that call into question the power of some of the core skills of the salesperson? For example the relationship-building skills of the salesperson, or the seller's ability to influence and persuade?

The spreadsheet-wielding, business case-building buyer with an almost insatiable appetite for information, and a set of rules and procedures to follow is scary for the seller. Perhaps that is why some sellers are in denial of their existence.

However, our research suggests that selling to the more hard-nosed numbers-driven buyer presents as many opportunities for sellers as it does challenges. It builds up existing sales skills rather than making them redundant. For example, it does not undermine the importance of building relationships and rapport with the buyer. Rather such rapport is important if the buyer is to get close enough to talk with the buyer about his numbers, business drivers and so on.

It does not diminish the seller's role, but rather expands it greatly, offering the hope of greater access, engagement and influence with the buyer. In particular the ability of the salesperson to add new value over and above the product or service they are selling, by helping the buyer to gather the numbers and do the analysis that will be required to justify the decision.

In the context of the three types of buyer, sellers must adopt a middle way – they must appeal to the instincts as well as the logic of the buyer. They must blend logic and emotion in how they sell. They must engage logic and analysis in building a compelling reason to buy. They must help the buyer to build the business case.

Buyers Are Rarely 100% Logical-Analytical

Buyers are people not computers and that makes them vulnerable to the normal human foibles in respect of decisions made. Buyers can jump to conclusions, be selective in the gathering of information, or biased in its interpretation. Indeed there are a variety of ways in which even the professional manager or buyer is bounded in their rationality.

Buyers are not as rational and analytical as their procurement policies and procedures would suggest. Indeed as science clearly demonstrates **the notion of the 100% logical analytical buyer is an illusion**. Even in the interpretation of core elements of the business case, such as the cost / benefits and risk, instinct or emotion has an important role to play.

All our research shows that it is not a question of whether buying decisions are 100% rational, or analytical, but whether they are 90%, 95% or 99% rational / analytical and 1%, 5% or 10% emotional, intuitive, or impulsive. Of course this very much depends on the nature of the purchase and the environment in which it is taking place. The modern IT salesperson appeals to logic and emotion equally. That means they help the buyer to reason their way to making the decision. They build the business case for what they sell.

11: Preventing Stalled Deals

Introduction

One of the most powerful realizations for IT vendors and internal project sponsors is that when it comes to the complex sale **there are no buying decisions, only business decisions**.

The implication is that buying decisions, which in the past focused on the 'What? 'Where? 'When?' and 'How?', are now more concerned with the 'Why?' For example:

- Why is this needed?
- Why should the company spend its time, energy and resources on this project or purchase?
- Why is this project or purchase necessary to improve the performance of our business?
- Why should this project or purchase be funded over another?
- Why can't this spending be put-off or cut?

If managers cannot answer 'why?' questions (such as those listed above) then they are not entitled to spend the company's money. Asking managers the 'why?' question is key to controlling spending, managing budgets and ensuring value for money.

If the 'why' question is not asked before the manager spends the money on a particular project, purchase or supplier then it could well be asked afterwards. Regardless **managers must be able to justify their decisions**. They must be able to answer the 'why' questions.

The manager's answer to the 'why' question may be given verbally or by means of a written document, a set of fields in a procurement system, or presented in front of a committee. Regardless it must be sufficiently solid or compelling as to be able to withstand scrutiny and to shatter resistance.

If the 'why?' questions are important for the buyer, they are important for the seller too. The problem is that they are too often being overlooked.

Most salespeople are busy telling their customers WHAT to buy and don't spend enough time explain WHY they should buy.

A Need Is Not Enough!

Traditionally the answer to the 'why buy this?' question was 'there is a need'. Today that is no longer adequate.

There may be a need – one for which the perfect technical solution has been identified. However that won't satisfy most budget-conscious managers.

Organizations, departments, projects, managers and indeed end users have lots of needs. But **only a small proportion of those needs command a budget**. That is not because the right solution or the best supplier cannot be identified. Rather it is because the business imperative or 'why' has not been established.

Why Projects and Purchases Stall

The number one reason why projects and purchases slow or stall is the lack of a compelling 'why'. Another word for this is the lack of a compelling business case justification. The mere fact that there is a demonstrable need is not enough. The implication for sellers is clear – look beyond the need and build a compelling justification for the purchase.

IT projects or purchases don't stall because the buyer cannot select a supplier. That is an obvious, yet very important statement of reality. Indeed it is worth repeating: **'Big projects don't stall**

because the buyer cannot select a supplier'. The implication is that sellers who focus on their competitive advantages over other suppliers are out of synch with the greatest challenge facing the buyer.

The modern IT salesperson is a 'why guy', rather than a 'technology guy'. He or she spends less time talking about 'how it works' and more time talking about 'why it is needed'. It is the difference between talking results and talking features and it has a major impact on closing the sale.

The Business behind Buying

Most IT buying decisions cannot be made unless the underlying business rationale or justification has been clearly demonstrated. So, behind every major IT purchasing decision, and many smaller ones too, is an important business decision. It is much more complex than the issues of technology features or supplier capability.

The business decision is more concerned with the 'why' or business rationale of the decision, while the buying decision is often more concerned with the 'how'. That is to say, the business decision is focused on results and outcomes. That is the business **impact of the IT purchase on the performance of a task, a function, project, business unit, facility, etc.** The question is: Does how you sell take this into account?

Justifying any IT project or purchase depends on an analysis of the costs and benefits. It also requires addressing factors such as risk, compliance and strategic fit.

Taking the Risk out of IT Decisions

Projects and purchases that are not supported by a robust business case justification are vulnerable to being stalled or scrapped. This can happen at any stage during the project lifecycle.

An IT project that is not backed up by a solid business case is at risk in the following ways:

- **Internal approvals** – the project may fail to get sanctioned by senior management. For example where questions about the payback or justification are not answered convincingly

- **Competing projects** – when it comes to accessing funds the project or purchase may lose out to another which has a more compelling business case. This can even happen where a budget has been provisionally allocated

- **Internal scrutiny** – All too often there is somebody from Finance or Procurement ready to pull holes in the numbers or the analysis and thereby stump the decision

- **Non-compliance** – increasingly there are internal procurement rules and procedures to be followed. If these are not complied with a purchase decision may be scuppered

- **Risk of project failure** – the old adage says 'failing to plan means planning to fail'. The business case is a risk management process, as well as a framework for improved decision-making, that enables managers to identify and manage project risk

- **Exposure of the manager** – the manager who fails to follow internal procurement procedures (or simply good practice) in making the decision is left exposed in the event that the project fails, as well as to allegations of sloppy decision-making or even favoritism.

- **Stakeholder support** – failure to build a proper business case for the IT investment decision is a lost opportunity to engage with and align stakeholders. This failure to ensure stakeholder buy-in and ownership is particularly important in political or high profile projects. Engaging stakeholders in the business case is also important to managing their expectations and the smooth adoption of any new systems, or technologies.

Focusing on the Business Decision

Buyers should not buy software or hardware unless it makes clear business sense. So the seller who wants to win the sale must help the buyer to establish the business rationale behind the purchase.

Focusing on justifying the business decision behind buying results in a major overhaul of traditional features and benefits selling. The salesperson who helps shape the business decision has reached the pinnacle of selling. Such high-level sales professionals are characterized by the following behaviors:

- Talk results
- Talk to more senior decision-makers
- Talk to non-technical buyers
- Ask better questions
- Connect with goals and strategies
- Face the real competition
- Don't assume the 'why?' is clear
- Pay attention to what could prevent a decision.

Let us examine each of these in turn.

1. Talk Results

The IT salesperson focused on facilitating the business decision is having much more interesting conversations, by:

- Talking about results before talking about technology features and benefits
- Packing sales materials and presentations with details of results achieved by other customers
- Quantifying results using the key metrics of interest to the buyer (cost per transaction, cost per data access point, cost per health and safety breach)
- Helping the buyer model the likely results to highlight what can be achieved in their business.

Talking results may require that salespeople take a crash course in basic accounting principles (see **Appendix**). Moreover salespeople quite literally need a calculator to sell – marketing adjectives in praise of the vendor's software or hardware are no longer enough – today's buyers need numbers.

2. Talk to More Senior Decision-makers

The IT salesperson who focuses on the business decision behind the purchase is talking to more interesting people. He or she is not just happy to engage with those in the IT department, or those at the lower levels, but wants to engage with people who have the authority to make business decisions, to shape priorities and to allocate budgets. They are increasingly talking to **C-level** managers — to the CEO, the CFO or the board.

But such high-level executives are not easy to access or engage. They don't meet very many salespeople and tend to be shielded by PAs and lower level managers. If they are to be engaged then different topics of conversation are likely to be required, including the issues of results, risks, compliance – the stuff of the business case. In **Chapter 14** we examine the language of the C-Level conversation.

3. Talk to Non-Technical Buyers

In focusing on the IT business decision, the salesperson talks with financial and business stakeholders, not just with the technical buyer. That means spending more time engaging with a more diverse group of stakeholders and a more cross-functional buying team.

The salesperson must seek out the business analyst acting as the bridge between technical or operational aspects of the purchase and the business case. If such a role does not exist it is particularly important that the salesperson helps to compensate for its absence. That means ensuring both business and technical sides of the buying organization are reconciled around a common business case and solution.

4. Ask Better Questions

Traditionally the salesperson asked questions aimed at understanding what was required to win the purchase order. These questions are shown on the left column of the table overleaf. Although still important in the context of modern buying, these questions are no longer enough because they fail to look beyond the buying decision to the business decision that underpins it

The salesperson who focuses on the business decision involved in buying IT asks better questions of the customer or prospect — those shown on the right-hand-side of the table below. These questions go to the core of the business decision. They uncover the real needs and most powerfully match them to the seller's solutions.

Buying Decisions *versus* Business Decision Questions

BUYING DECISION QUESTIONS	BUSINESS DECISION QUESTIONS
What is the criterion for the ideal solution?	What is the business case?
What features do you want?	What are the objectives?
What is the criterion for the best supplier?	How does it fit with our strategy?
What is the budget?	How will it improve performance?
Where is the budget coming out from?	What are all the options and alternatives?
What is the desired feature set?	What is the expected payback?
What are the specifications?	What is the total cost of ownership?
How long before a decision is made?	What are the risks?
What are the best terms?	What people and process issues exist?
What is the 'best deal'?	How will we ensure implementation success?
How will it be delivered?	What are our peers in other companies doing?
Who will sign the order?	Have the stakeholders agreed?
What paperwork is required?	Will senior managers sign it off?
	Are there competing projects?

Sellers who cannot see behind the technology buying decision to the business decision that underlies it ask the wrong questions (those on the left) and it hinders their success. Simply asking better questions (those on the right) can transform the buyer-seller conversation – it can result in a new level of influence and engagement for the salesperson.

In **Chapter 15** we examine the most powerful of all the questions that the seller can use to connect with the buyer's business justification for the purchase.

5. Connect with Goals and Strategies

An ability to see the business dimension of the IT project or purchase requires an understanding of the buyer's business and industry. It also requires connecting with the business goals and strategies of the buying organization.

In particular, it draws attention to the top priorities, including the drive to cut costs, increase efficiency and minimizing risk. It also brings into focus the business drivers and constraints that impact on the sale, including people, politics, culture and strategic fit (see **Part 1**).

6. Face The Real Competition

Sellers who focus on the buying decision for hardware, software or SaaS realize that the main competition today is often not another vendor, but another project or course of action within the buying organization.

With scarce organizational resources, businesses must make choices between projects, priorities and strategies that are competing for the same resources.

The job of the salesperson is to help the sponsor or buyer to make their particular IT project more compelling than the alternatives, including a decision to do the work in-house, to choose an alternative technology or the most common decision of all — to delay making a decision.

7. Don't Assume the 'Why?' Is Clear

It can be dangerous to assume that the business rationale for the decision is clear and that it is compelling. This happens when sellers:

- Assume that the buyer knows what he or she is trying to achieve, or has clear goals or objectives for the IT project or purchase

- Absolutely believe in their product and what it can do – so much so that they don't realize that others may not have the same belief.

If you start with an automatic unquestioned assumption that buying your solution is the 'right' thing to do, then you are only building the business case to justify what you have already decided. In short you are prejudiced. So, rather than saying 'this is compelling', ask 'is this compelling?' When you do you will:

- Act in the role of a consultant or coach, rather than just a salesperson

- Overcome skepticism and the comment 'you are only saying that because you want to sell to us'

- Get the buyer thinking for himself or herself and focus attention on what is required to justify the decision

- Prequalify the opportunity in terms of how advanced it really is and also how senior the buyer (or your contact) is.

8. Pay Attention to What Could Prevent A Decision

That leads us to is another somewhat unconventional, but effective way to use the business case to prevent a stalled project or deal. It starts with looking for what could go wrong and then working to prevent it from happening.

If you understand why the project or purchase might not get sanctioned, then you are in a much better position to convincingly communicate why it should.

So, for each of the key headings of the business case (cost / benefits and risk) identify the reasons why the decision might stall. For example:

- If the decision was to stall on the basis of the numbers (the economics) why would that be? Would it be because a payback within 12 months is required, or because the numbers presented were not believed by Finance?

- If risk was to stall the decision, why would that be? Would it be because of unaddressed concerns or missing information? What type of risks most concern the buyer – supplier risk, technical risk, project risk, etc?

You can think of it as a deal pre-mortem that focuses on 'What could go wrong?' as opposed to a deal post-mortem that asks 'Why did it go wrong?'. By the time the post-mortem of a lost deal is undertaken it is too late. But by anticipating what could go wrong the seller can prepare for – and prevent – it before it happens.

Approaching the issue of the business case in this way helps the sponsor / seller to avoid making what is one of the key mistakes in preparing the business case – that is to assume there is one.

The New Needs Analysis

Make questions about the business justification required for a decision an integral part of your needs analysis or fact-find. It is every bit as important as the assessment of technical requirements, definition of the problem and so on. Such questions include:

- How **important** is the decision?

- Is a **business case** required? What form will it take?

- What are the underlying **business drivers, strategies and goals**?
- What level of **financial analysis** will be involved?
- What kind of **payback/ROI** is required?
- What are the **relevant KPIs and metrics**?
- What are the **costs** (including full life costs) and **benefits**?
- What is **the level of risk** inherent in the decision?
- Are there **other projects** competing for the same resources?
- Are there **strategic alternatives** available to the buyer?
- How does the purchase **fit with previous decisions**, existing processes and people?
- What are the **political** issues?
- Are there any **compliance** and governance issues?

Take an opportunity or deal in your pipeline and see how many of the above questions you can answer. Circle any questions that present a challenge and note the actions that are required to find the answer. Doing this has the potential to really help you accelerate the deal in question.

How do you present your prospect / the buyer with a compelling reason to buy? The answer is the business case. It is about turning marketing plea into economic justification. It is about providing the buyer with a compelling reason to buy – one that can withstand the scrutiny that is required in resource-strapped organizations. It is about helping the buyer to make the right decision for the right reason and shaping the logical / rational economic basis for it.

12: The Naked IT Sales Proposal

Introduction

Many sellers are leaving their buyers naked! They are getting them excited about their technology solutions and then letting them go off unprepared to their senior management colleagues looking for purchase approval.

Traditional sales approaches send buyers into management and even board meetings without the basics in terms of the justification required to get a 'go-ahead'. The risk for the buyer is embarrassment, for the seller it is a stalled deal.

Are You Leaving Your Buyer Naked?

Vendors have been slow to realize that the role of the sales pitch or proposal goes well beyond selling a technology or solution. Helping the buyer to get the purchase or project sanctioned is part of the job too.

With this in mind here is the real test of the powerful sales proposal:

Can the buyer use it to get the purchase approved?

More to the point, can he or she present it directly to his or her senior management colleagues to justify the purchase decision? We call this the 'Naked Proposal' test.

The Two Decisions

Many buyers are being left naked in the face of buying committees and senior management reviews. That is in spite of the seller's efforts in preparing many pages of neatly designed proposals and other documentation.

Most vendor proposals fall short of satisfying the needs of senior managers, **especially those from Finance or Procurement.** They are not enough to justify a decision because they are focused on the secondary, as opposed to the primary, decision for the buyer.

The Primary Decision

Buyers tell us time and time again that **choosing a supplier is not the most difficult part of the decision.** Their biggest challenges are to wrestle scarce resources for their project and to ensure that they are not waylaid by competing internal priorities, budget cuts, or politics. That is the primary decision.

The primary decision is to go ahead and to go ahead now. It is the decision to spend the money on this, as opposed to something else. Everything else is secondary.

> In the results-oriented bottom line-driven organization the business case is Gospel, not the 'love the neighbor – all are blessed' Gospel but the Old Testament message of 'only the good will flourish'. It is the essential means by which those **IT projects and purchases most deserving of resources** are ruthlessly separated from the rest.

The Secondary Decision

The reason why deals get stalled is not because the buyer cannot choose another supplier, but because he fails to get the decision sanctioned or the resources allocated – resources for which other purchases, projects, or departments may be vying.

Selecting a supplier in most cases is only a secondary decision. It must be preceded by a decision to go ahead with the project or the purchase in the first instance.

Yet it is the secondary decision that most sales proposals are aimed at influencing. They focus on the secondary 'why choose us?' decision, as opposed to answering the more fundamental 'why do this?' question.

If the seller is to be certain of winning the sale the sales proposal must help the buyer to get the go ahead for the purchase or project. That is a tall order for the salesperson's proposal and it is exactly what the 'Naked Proposal' test is all about.

> The business case is one of the **greatest forms of competitive differentiation**, not just of the salesperson, but of his / her solution. The salesperson who can meaningfully input to the buyer's business case is clearly in pole position.

Why Proposals Don't Get Sanctioned

Why can't buyers take the seller's proposal and use it to get the purchase decision sanctioned? That is a question we have asked of both buyers and sellers.

Many sellers suggest initially that **the typical proposal is too long** for the buyer to put in front of their colleagues to get the decision approved. But if that is the reason then surely the buyer could take the executive summary and use it to get the decision sanctioned. That means there must be another reason.

On reflection IT vendors then admit that their proposals were **not written for the purpose of getting the purchase sanctioned**. Little wonder then that buyers are not using them for that purpose.

The buyer is likely to take some of what is in the seller's proposal, but a lot of what it contains is not the stuff that gets the decision sanctioned. But if that is the case then surely there is something wrong with the way that IT sales proposals are written? The answer has to be 'yes'.

The seller's proposal must present a compelling rationale for the purchase, counter all the potential objections that are likely to be raised and answer the questions that are likely to arise. If it does not then it is a case of 'the emperor has no clothes'.

Well-written, glossy proposals are a folly unless they present a logical and compelling argument for the IT vendor's solution – one that is capable of withstanding scrutiny from within as well as without.

*Salespeople want to communicate influence and persuade buyers. But when it comes to helping the buyer to make the decision they often adopt a peculiarly hands-off role. That is because when it comes to actually making the decision so much of what they seek to **influence, persuade and communicate** about is peripheral to the real basis for the decision being made. That is the business rationale for making the decision, or what we like to call the business case.*

Sales Proposals – What's Missing?

The reality is that most IT sales proposals do not address the fundamental question every buyer needs answered: 'How will this IT project or purchase increase the performance of the customer's business?'. That means they fall short of providing the key information required in order to get a purchase approved.

To be effective a sales proposal has to demonstrate how the solution will help the buyer to achieve the results that his or her business, project, or team requires. Put another way it has to demonstrate a compelling business case – that is a compelling case for buying. That is what is required to help the buyer to decide or, if a decision has already been made, to justify it.

The proposal or tender must give the buyer the ammunition required to sell your solution when you are not in the room. It must show the impact on the key relevant business / project performance metrics, a compelling cost / benefits analysis, address the issue of risk, strategic fit and compliance. If it does not then it is the equivalent of the buyer being caught with his or her trousers down.

> If a business case can put a project in pole position then what can it do for a supplier? **If it is the basis on which projects compete then it should be the basis on which suppliers compete too.** It should be the basis on which the seller separates himself / herself from the rest.

Mind the Language In Your Proposal!

We analyzed a sample of 30 randomly-chosen IT vendor sales proposals by copying the text they contained and putting it into a word cloud using Wordle.net. The results are below, with the biggest words being the most commonly used within sales proposals.

The message from vendors is a 'Me! Me! Me!' one. It is sellers bragging about their products and pedigree, for example:

- 'We were established in 1993'
- 'We have offices in London and New York'
- We employ 5,000 people and have ISO certification'
- 'We won most innovative product award in 2014'.

Of course there is a lot of marketing-created product features and benefits information too.

This traditional vendor information has a role to play. Sellers are rightly proud of their products and other achievements, especially where these are a clear differentiator over competitors. The only problem is that sellers overestimate how important messages are for the buyer.

What is clear from the analysis of proposals is that IT vendors are not using the language of the business case. Nowhere in the list above are words such as economics, cost / benefits analysis, risk, compliance, or strategic fit for example. That makes it a great opportunity for you!

The challenge for sellers is to embrace the business case-related vocabulary of the senior business executive involved in approving so many of today's IT decisions. We will take up this point again in the next two chapters where the buyer's vocabulary is explored in some detail.

> The business case is the road less travelled when it comes to selling IT. If you want to distance yourself from other sellers it is the only route to take.

Sales Proposals – The New Table of Contents

Let us compare the structure of the typical IT vendor proposal to the structure of the buyer's business case or purchase approvals document.

The typical salesperson's proposal focuses on the following key headings:

- Problem
- Solution
- Benefits / Features
- Cost
- Team, Company and Credentials.

However, this is out of synch with the structure of the buyer's business case, which requires information under the following key headings:

- Economic analysis — Cost / Benefits
- Risk analysis
- Strategic rationale
- Recommendation
- Implementation.

The proposal and the business case are two very different documents. Little wonder then that vendor proposals often miss the mark.

As we saw in **Part 1** the buyer's thought process around buying IT is a sophisticated one. The problem is that many traditional IT sales proposals are not as sophisticated. In particular they often neglect the key issues of economics, strategy and risk that can result in a 'go', or 'no go' buying decision.

The business case is the most important argument for winning the sale – the most logical and compelling. It is the $E=MC^2$ of why the buyer needs your solution.

The Proposal – Business Justification Test

Here is a test to help you measure your proposal in terms of how well it communicates the business justification for your solution:

- **Take the binding** off a recent proposal
- Put the **pages in bundles** – one for each of the five elements of the value equation: cost / benefits, risk and so on
- **Count the pages** in each bundle and express them as a percentage of the total proposal (risk – 0.5 pages or 2% of the proposal). Put the answers in the visual overleaf
- Compare the breakdown of your proposal with the expected weighting of each factor in the **buyer's decision criteria** (risk is likely to have a 20% weighting for the buyer, but we only gave it 2% of our proposal)
- **Rewrite the table of contents** to address those areas of the value equation that are not being dealt with fully by your proposal / pitch – they could greatly add to your overall value.

Communicating your value to today's hard-nosed buyers can be a real challenge. You know that your marketing literature won't do it. So your sales pitches and proposals must. There is a key test of how well you can do it – it is 'to write the last page first'.

> Helping the buyer to build a compelling business case for the purchase is **the number one job of the modern salesperson**. That means not just rewriting sales proposals in the language of the business case, but lots more instead. It requires a transition from sales proposition to business proposition and from salesperson to business person who sells.

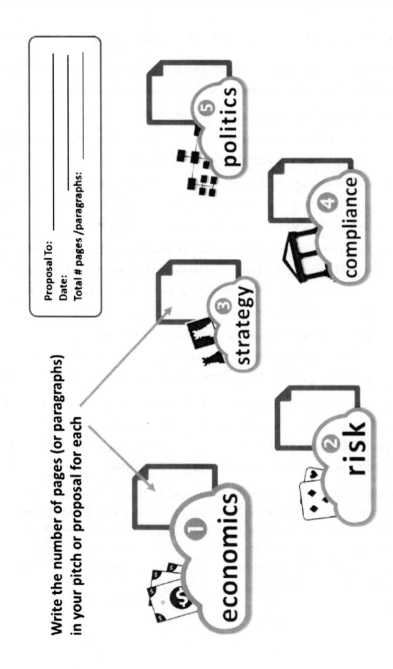

Write the number of pages (or paragraphs) in your pitch or proposal for each

Proposal To:
Date:
Total # pages / paragraphs:

1 economics

2 risk

3 strategy

4 compliance

5 politics

Write the Last Page First

Have you ever noticed that buyers have an infuriating habit of starting to read from the back, as opposed to the front, of the sales proposal? They want numbers and are impatient to get them. This is something that sellers often underestimate in writing their proposals.

Most vendor proposals are shy on metrics — at least the key metrics of interest to senior managers. Indeed, often the only quantifiable data relates to cost. The last few pages of the sales proposal sheepishly deliver a price tag and that is it!

Sellers' proposals should provide a robust justification of the investment that is required on the part of the buyer. They must put the ROI on the first page of their proposals in a prominent position in the executive summary. This goes a long way to putting clothes on your sales proposal.

As we will see in **Chapter 16** sellers need a calculator to help today's more sophisticated buyers. However, putting the numbers and the business logic for the decision right up at the very front of your pitches and proposals is a real test of confidence for the seller.

13: The Beermat Business Case

beermat
business case

$ € ¥ £
$ € ¥ £
$ € ¥ £

www.SellingintheClouds.com

Introduction

Being able to build the business case for your IT solution is an important **sales skill**. However the traditional approach to developing the business case fails more often than it succeeds.

To address this problem sellers need to start the business case conversation much earlier. They need to adopt what can be called 'beermat' business case principles. The message is clear – **don't wait till all the data is available, or the proposal is being prepared,** before starting to sketch out the business case with the customer.

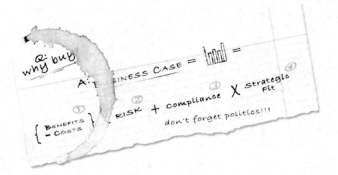

Have You Got All The Sales Tools You Need?

OK, so you have a complete sales kit for your sales meetings with customers and prospects. It includes:

- Product samples
- Customer testimonials
- Glossy brochures
- Case studies
- Technical FAQs.

You even have before and after pictures! But what are you missing? Numbers, or more to the point a simple means of sketching out some key aspects of the business case from the initial customer contact. That is not a typical ROI calculator, however – it is too early for that!

At the earlier stages of the sale it is generally easier to get the buyer to react to a simple generic model than to share all the required information or to input to a detailed ROI calculator. This is where the idea of the 'beermat' business case comes in.

The Business Case on a Beermat

The Beermat Entrepreneur was a popular book written by Mike Southon and Chris West a number of years ago. It was a simple, yet clever idea – that you should be able to communicate your business idea in so clear and concise a manner as to fit on the back of a beermat!

Yes an entrepreneur needs a detailed business plan (just as the salesperson is going to need to prepare a proposal or tender), but the essentials of the proposition **should be so clear as to be communicated on a space no bigger than a beermat**. This principle is nowhere more relevant than in selling IT to the hard-nosed business buyer.

The business case for IT was seen traditionally as complex and perhaps even intimidating. It required a lot of information and analysis. However, these views don't help either the vendor, or the internal sponsor who wants to build and communicate a compelling business justification for buying new hardware, software or cloud-based computing.

Why the Business Case Can't Wait

Typically developing the business case is done late in the sales cycle, perhaps even at the proposal stage. It often results in the buyer being presented with a *fait accompli* business case to which he or she has had little real input. That limits its power to win the sale in at least three ways:

- **You can't present somebody with a compelling business case.** It is not going to be compelling unless they are engaged, unless they are involved in its creation. Even if the buyer embraces a business case you give them, chances are they won't be able to defend it if required. So, rather than giving somebody your business case, help them to build their own. That requires a lot more time and patience, but it is the only way it will work

- **You probably have had to make a lot of assumptions** in order to prepare a detailed business case. The risk is that any one of these might be easily rejected by the buyer. When it comes to the early stage business case it is better to be approximately right than exactly wrong. That means keeping the business case simple to start with

- **The business case is a shot in the dark unless there has been a dialogue** between buyer and seller. It can be easy for the seller to overlook aspects of the business case that may be politically sensitive, or perhaps even a 'no go area'. For example, a managed service in respect of IT support might boast the benefits of reducing IT overheads; however with up to 30% of those overheads being accounted for by IT staff salaries, cutting staff numbers may be problematic. Unless a dialogue has taken place around the business case such sensitivities may not be obvious.

The advice for sellers is: don't wait till all the numbers come in, or until the buyer is ready to open up and disclose all the information.

If you leave the cost / benefits analysis till the end then it is too late. If you wait to present the customer with a complete business case, with lots of calculations and formulas, the likelihood is that it won't be believed.

The Business Case Conversation

The challenge is to engage in the business case conversation right from the very outset of the sale. You can't wait to talk about numbers until you have all the data that you need.

You cannot wait until the customer is ready to open up and share his or her numbers with you. You certainly cannot wait to the point of submitting a proposal!

The earlier you can engage with the buyer around the business case, the quicker you can move the conversation off price and onto value and the more effectively you can out-flank the competition.

The quicker you can get to the business case the greater your chances of success.

A good business case should be easily communicated and developed on the fly. It should follow beermat principles.

It Is Never Too Early to Talk Business Case

The business case is not just a document or a spreadsheet. It has to be a dialogue. Yes, that is a challenge where access to senior executives and to information is limited. However the challenge can be overcome by applying these five principles:

- **Get in early with the business case** and in particular with the numbers. Plant the seeds of the business case right from the very initial conversation. Indeed don't talk about a benefit or feature of your solution, without referring to its impact on key business or project metrics that are likely to interest the buyer

- **Start with a hypothesis of value**, with scenarios and assumptions. Keep it clear, focus on only one or two key metrics or variables. Hold off on the detail and the spreadsheets until later

- **Make the calculation clear** and spell out the assumptions. Above all, state that it is only a quick calculation and would need a lot more work. Where possible back it up with some verifiable data, as well as some anecdotal customer stories

- **Don't assume there is a strong business case**, before it is proven. This is at the core of being a trustworthy adviser and it requires replacing your benefit statements with benefit questions. Ask the buyer more questions such as 'do you think there is a compelling business case at this time?', or 'what would make a compelling business case for this solution?'

- **Hold off on the ROI calculator.** It is a great tool, but at the early stages of the sale it is often the wrong tool. That is because it can bias, perhaps even side-track, the conversation. It often makes assumptions and takes the initiative away from the buyer. So slow down before you take out the ROI calculator.

Use your beermat business case to gauge how much the numbers (the business case) actually matter to the prospect and whether the decision requires an economic justification. It is a powerful means of qualifying the buyer and the likelihood of a decision. For example, if the buyer is not interested in talking numbers, then:

- He or she may not be sufficiently senior
- The buying decision may not be as advanced as you had imagined.

Start with a Hypothesis

Tease the buyer with some simple examples, key metrics and customer stories. They are the stuff of the beermat business case. But don't present them as a universal truth, or even as a certainty. Gauge the reaction to see which ones actually have relevance to the buyer's business.

At the early stages of the sale your business case is a hypothesis, rather than a statement of fact. So, preface any claims or benefit statements with 'other customers have achieved', 'the industry rule of thumb is …', or 'analysts suggest'. Here is an example:

Some companies have achieved between 3% and 7% reduction in downtime. How might such figures apply in your business?

Let the buyer pick holes in the data if required. In so doing they are helping you to better understand the metrics that are most relevant to their business – the metrics to use in their business case.

It is important to **distinguish between a real business case and a mere hypothesis of value**. Now, there is nothing intrinsically wrong with a hypothesis – as long as it is not attempting to masquerade as anything more than that.

Until ownership of the business case transfers from seller to buyer, any metrics presented are no more than scenarios, or hypotheses. Vendors therefore cannot simply present a spreadsheet model as a *fait accompli* business case.

On at least some level, every manager / buyer views his or her business and its situation as being different; this means that industry benchmarks and case studies will tend to be more interesting than compelling. However, what others have or have not achieved is simply another example of a hypothesis.

> *In selling to the business case the destination is the same – a purchase order for your solution. But the journey to get there is a lot more interesting. It is safer too. And hopefully the buyer is along for the most of the journey. That way you don't find yourself at what you thought was the finish line only to discover that the buyer has gone somewhere else.*

Start with Modest Numbers

It is always important to bear in mind that the highest vendor ROI does not necessarily secure the sale. This is largely because, as buyers are quick to point out, **'justifying the purchase is a lot more demanding than justifying the sale'**.

Meanwhile, vendor ROI metrics tend to come with a **'WARNING!'** label. This is especially true when we consider the following rules of thumb:

- The more questions you ask then the fewer guesses and assumptions you need to make and therefore the more chance you have of 'hitting the mark'
- The less somebody is involved in preparing an ROI model, the more quickly he or she will distance himself or herself from it
- The bigger the claim, the more easily it can be discredited
- The more variables involved in an ROI model, the greater the likelihood of one of them being disputed.

Build It Slowly

As with building skyscrapers, the temptation for sellers in building a business case (or any metrics) for the buyer is to add another floor of benefits in a bid to achieve the highest possible ROI for the buyer. However, it is important to remember that the higher the ROI, the greater the danger of the buyer simply toppling your figures.

Many buyers express a preference for more modest vendor ROI claims. Below are some comments from buyers that help to explain this reality:

- A vendor coming in and saying that he / she can cut costs by 10% and increase turnover by 20% is going to elicit one or both of the following reactions from the prospective buyer:
  - That is simply **not credible** (If it was really that simple, we would have done it ourselves long ago)
  - What you are basically saying is that **I have not been doing my job properly** – that in respect of key measures (costs and turnover), I am somewhere between 10% and 20% below par

- **Be careful what you take credit for** in terms of what you are claiming your solution will do for the buyer. Vendors have a tendency to succumb to the temptation of quantifying every possible benefit – including those that should not ordinarily be quantified, or those that are only indirectly attributable to the vendor's solution.

*Sellers need to focus as much on developing the business case as they do on **developing relationships in order to win the sale**. They need to develop their relationship with the buyer's numbers goals, numbers and strategies ...*

Don't Wait until You Are Sure

Building the business case is not easy. Otherwise every seller would be doing it and doing it well. However, if the seller struggles in building the business case, then chances are the customer will struggle too.

So, don't be put off by gaps or uncertainties and don't wait until you are sure of everything. The business case must be a process of discovery with questions as well as answers.

Struggling with the business case is only a problem if it happens at the closing stage of the sale. If at the end of the process the buyer is still struggling with the economic justification for the purchase, or the purchase of your solution in particular, then the decision is likely to falter.

Up to the point of closing it is OK to struggle with the business case. Indeed if it is not creating a certain amount of struggle then it is probably not getting the attention it needs.

Sellers shouldn't be shy of saying the business case requires time and attention. They should not feel under pressure to produce a business case 'out of the hat'.

Don't Wait until the Customer Is Ready

Start to sketch out the beermat business case, even if the customer doesn't appear to be interested or ready. The business case is the rationale for the purchase; if it is not required today, it could be essential tomorrow.

If the business case conversation is left until the sales cycle is advanced, then there is the risk that it will take place without the salesperson being involved. When this happens the danger is that the buyer will say 'we have our own business case, but the information contained therein is confidential'.

Obviously one concern that the buyer will have is that any costs used will set the expectations of the seller regarding price and therefore prevent a competitive tender.

Getting involved earlier in the business case conversation is **an important defensive move** for the seller. Buying decisions take place in an environment of continuous flux. A change in priorities, a competing project, a decision at HQ, or a change in key personnel can stall the project. In these situations the business case may be the only hope of survival.

Getting involved earlier in the business case conversation **means being proactive**. After all, why delay in providing the buyer with the most powerful and persuasive technique there is – the rational economic justification for the decision? Even if the buyer does not seem too concerned about the numbers, or the justification, the issue is likely to arise sooner or later.

Getting involved earlier in the business case conversation is a powerful way of connecting what you are selling with what the customer is trying to achieve. In particular it is a way of connecting with the **customer's strategy**, business drivers and so on. And it means that the seller has the prospect of getting involved earlier and shaping requirements.

Warning: You Don't Own the Business Case!

Sellers cannot leave it up to the customer to do the math. The buyer may not have the time or the tools, information and experience required to build a credible and compelling set of numbers – one that won't simply fall to pieces when it is exposed to questioning.

However, the seller must be careful about taking control of the business case from the buyer.

Buyers are told 'Don't believe the seller's ROI. Build your own'. That is a principle sellers should accept. Even if the buyer is struggling with the business case, don't be tempted to jump in and take over. The seller must help, but at the end of the day the buyer has to own the business case.

> *What is the point in knowing how many children the buyer has and what football team they support, if the seller does not know the buyer's key business drivers related to the purchase? The seller needs to get into the sacred space of talking about the business case with the buyer.*

Does the Buyer Own the Business Case?

How does the seller know whether the buyer has truly embraced the business case? This is of vital importance.

It is very easy for the buyer to nod politely in agreement with the business case and its numbers when talking to the salesperson. But it is another thing entirely for the buyer to take the business case down the hall to his colleagues and superiors and justify it with confidence and conviction. The difference between the two is the level of ownership of the business case by the buyer.

Here is a key test of whether ownership has passed from seller to buyer:

- When the buyer talks about the business case does he or she refer to it as 'theirs', or 'yours'?

If the buyer refers to the business case as the seller's (rather than their own) then it is a sign that ownership has not passed and that there is more work still to be done. More engagement and more co-creation is going to be required if the seller is to maintain his or her influence over the decision.

Here is another test of both buyer ownership and readiness in term of the business case. It is to ask:

- Who have you shown the business case to?
- What reaction did you get?

If the buyer has **not** shown the business case to others yet, then ask:

- Do you think you are ready to share your business case?

The answers to these questions reveal a lot about the business case ownership and confidence of the buyer.

Here are some questions to help you probe where exactly the buyer is at in terms of the business case justification:

- Do you feel that the business case as it is today is sufficiently clear and compelling?
- Are there aspects of the business case that you feel need more work?
- Do you feel confident in all the numbers – that they will withstand external scrutiny?
- What would the CFO think if he or she saw the business case at this time?

The seller who rushes ahead, oblivious to signs of anxiety or a lack of engagement on the part of the buyer, often ends up being disappointed. So, when it comes to the business case there is often a need for the seller to slow right down. The questions above will help you to gauge your speed.

Using Beermats to Win Over Stakeholders

It is not just the seller who needs to be able to articulate the business on a beermat. The buyer needs to be able to do so too. Many purchases are justified not in round table meetings, but in hallway encounters.

In the early stages at least, the buyer may not get a chance to go line by line through a spreadsheet. We regularly hear C-level executives telling their managers to put the business case on one page for them to review.

The buyer needs to be able to clearly articulate the business case whether it is just in a hallway encounter with a management colleague, or the last item on the agenda of a long meeting when everybody has lost attention.

The business case needs to be **capable of being communicated in tabloid headings and high level numbers**. For the buyer the business case has to be so clear (and compelling) as to be capable of being communicated on a beermat.

The challenge for the seller is to help the buyer to develop a level of comfort and confidence around the business justification as to be ample to communicate it on a beermat. That is quite an achievement, but one that exerts an unparalleled influence over the decision.

Take the Beermat Test

Take any of the top five opportunities in your pipeline and see if you can explain the business case for the buyer in no more than a few minutes using the blank beermat opposite.

14: Selling IT Business Impact

www.SellingintheClouds.com

Business Impact, not Technology Benefits!

There is a new rule in selling IT to the new buyer – **business impact before benefits**. If followed it has the potential to transform and indeed accelerate the traditional IT sale. However it is a rule that features and technology-obsessed IT vendors can't help but break.

The challenge we all face as sellers (of IT or anything else) is to find ways to connect what we sell with what the customer cares about most – the strategy, performance and results of their business, project, department or team. That cannot be done by listing the features and benefits of our technology. The focus has to be on business impact, as opposed to technology benefits.

The Sameness of Benefits

The reality is that when it comes to IT vendors and their benefits there is an uncanny sameness. Search through the web marketing of leading IT competitors and I bet you will quickly get lost in a sea of sameness.

Here are just two examples of the sameness of IT vendor messages:

- Of the 13 variables used to compare the solutions of the leading **IT network inventory solutions** vendors, only two of the criteria showed any real differences between the companies. In short all the vendors are making the same claims about their products, including reporting, detail level, speed, and so on. In fact, so much so that the average buyer could hardly tell one from another

- An analysis of six key vendors of **back-end policy administration solutions** shows that cloning happens across even the most established industries. All promise the same benefits (time to market, cutting administration costs, etc), as well as the same features (scalable, multi-language, etc). In fact, the degree of sameness was such that it is almost as if all the websites and brochures for all six vendors were written by the same people!

It can be very difficult for potential customers to tell one competitor from another based on traditional benefits messages they communicate. If you want to stand out, then something more is required.

Most IT Benefits Are Bland!

In the words of one buyer 'most benefits as promoted by vendors are bland'. In other words they are rarely compelling. Too often they present a technical rather than an economic or business argument for the product or solution involved.

Think of it this way – **traditional IT vendor benefits are like firecrackers**. They struggle to get the business buyer's attention and are quickly forgotten. On the other hand business impact is like dynamite. It can't but be heard and it has the power to blow a hole in inertia and resistance to change.

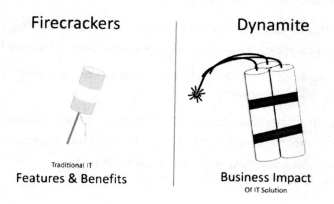

Firecrackers | Dynamite

Traditional IT
Features & Benefits | Business Impact
Of IT Solution

Traditionally the benefits of IT services, hardware or software, as found in glossy brochures and slick slide decks, were relevant to technical buyers alone. Most were not quantified, monetized or backed up with third party validation. Too often they resulted in a 'so what' as opposed to 'tell me more' response.

The table below compares the old and increasingly ineffective way of selling IT with the new approach focused on communicating business impact.

Comparing Old and New IT Messages

MESSAGE	OLD: BENEFITS	NEW: BUSINESS IMPACT
Quantified:	• No	• **Yes, Clear Metrics**
Validation:	• None, We Say So	• **Proven By Customers**
Focused on:	• Value Proposition	• **Buyer's Key Metrics**
Relevant to:	• 'Technical' Buyers	• **Senior Management**
Uniqueness:	• Similar To Others	• **Stands-Out**
Contained in:	• Marketing Brochures	• **Customer Case Studies**
Used in:	• Seller Sales Pitches	• **Buyer Business Case**
Reaction Got:	• 'So What!?'	• **'Tell Me More'**

Moving Beyond Old Benefits

Most salespeople struggle to move beyond adjectives in selling their solutions. This greatly limits their effectiveness. Here is an example:

Our customers achieve significant savings as a result of implementing our solutions …

That sounds pretty bland, right? 'Significant savings' is vague and somewhat unconvincing. It does not grab attention, or represent a compelling reason to buy, or at least explore buying.

Now change the message slightly, as follows:

> *Our customers, including companies A, B and C, have achievde savings of up to 20% as a result of implementing our solutions ...*

The impact is a lot greater, right? First off, there are companies mentioned, that adds credibility and third party validation. Then the benefits are made tangible, maybe even quantified. That tells customers exactly what to expect.

The conclusion: if you want to grab your prospect's attention and keep them reading – quantify the results that your solutions have achieved for other customers. The rest of the sales process is then focused on the salesperson and prospect exploring how he or she can achieve the same or a similar result.

Benefits Out, Business Impact In

Today's professional buyers want **answers that cannot be found in traditional marketing literature** or sales aids. They want metrics, not slogans. They want quantifiable data, not marketing adjectives. They want solid statements of business impact, not fluffy benefits and features presentations.

The new more business-focused buyer wants something they can put into a spreadsheet and calculate in terms of future revenues. They will sit up and pay attention to sellers who quantify results and back it up with third party validation.

Business impact gets the attention of senior business managers because it uses the buyer's performance metrics and customer validation to build a business case for the IT solution.

What Buyers Need to Hear

What is important to managers? Well, clearly results! Business impact is simply another word for results.

IT vendors who rely on the features and benefits of their technology to sell are not **telling buyers what they want to hear**. They need to stop explaining why their solutions are so great and instead show the impact that it can have on the customer's business. The bottom line is that IT vendors need to focus on their customer's results.

Some IT vendors can show an impact on the balance sheet or income statement of their customers, but that may not be always possible. Instead, the business impact may need to be measured at the level of:

- Particular departments, projects, facilities, or functions
- Specific processes, workflows or even tasks
- The achievement of particular milestones, metrics, or other results
- Specific stakeholders, or perhaps even end users.

How performance is measured will vary for managers at different levels, with different job titles and in different industries. But measuring is a necessity. The seller must understand the specific performance metrics that are relevant for the buying organization overall, as well as for the different buyer-managers and stakeholders.

Here is an example of one metric in respect of life and pensions policy administration solutions and the stakeholders concerned.

Using Metrics To Sell

Relevant Metric	Administration cost per policy
Who is watches this metric	CFO, COO, CEO, CTO
BEFORE Seller's Solution	£18.75
AFTER Seller's Solution	£12.15 (down 35%)
Validated by	Gartner based model, Qualex Case Study

*Communicate a compelling business case by means of your pitches and proposals. That is **high decibel sales and marketing**. The other won't even be heard, or if heard won't be remembered.*

The 'Before-After' Test

As a seller you need an unambiguous and compelling way to communicate the reason for buying your solution. That means you must be able to present **a before and after picture** in terms of the impact of their solution.

The 'before-after' comparison is a powerful technique long popular among ad agency executives. Either in print or on TV the approach is the same:

- First **the customer's present reality** is clearly shown, whether that is a stain on a carpet, a frustratingly slow Internet connection, or a shocking bill. The implications or consequences are made evident, so too is the emotional impact on the customer. The need for a solution is compellingly clear. That is the 'before'

- Then **the customer's problem or dilemma** is resolved before our eyes thanks to the marketer's solution. To follow our earlier examples the stain is gone, the Internet connection is

now lightning fast, or the customer can afford an extra
holiday because the bill has been reduced. Moreover the
customer is visibly appears confident, happy and secure. That
is the highly desirable 'after'.

The 'before-after' format is perhaps one of the simplest but yet
most powerful methods of communicating any sales or marketing
proposition. It can be used to powerful effect in selling IT.

Here is an example of this form of 'before-after' analysis in respect
of a back-end administration solution for an insurance company:

Customer A, Results Achieved

	Before	After	Change
Admin cost per policy	18	12	-33%
Time to Issue New Policy (days)	4	1	-75%
Cost of handling customer enquiry	3	1.5	-50%
Cost of policy amendment	4	2	-50%
New Policies Issued Weekly	2000	2200	10%
Enquiry to Policy Win Rate	50%	55%	10%
Time to market for new products (weeks)	6	2	-67%

The 'before' is the problem and the 'after' is the solution. By
contrasting the two the need for the seller's solution should become
demonstrably clear. If yours is not then where is the gap? Is it the
problem ('before') or the solution ('after') that you need to
communicate more effectively?

The Power of the 'Before-After'

There is a subtle yet powerful psychology involved in the 'before-after' analysis. It gets the buyer to focus not just on the opportunity or challenge they are facing, but also their desired future.

Helping the buyer to define success – in terms of the 'after' in the 'before-after' analysis – is a powerful sales technique. That is because it involves connecting your solution with the buyer's hopes and aspirations, their strategies and goals.

It offers the prospect of changing the conversation from one about product features and benefits to a conversation about business impact and results.

Creating Your 'Before-After'

Most IT vendors would never get a job in an advertising agency. That is because they struggle to present a 'before-after' analysis for their solutions. The minority who can are increasingly capturing the buyer's attention. With this in mind let's set about capturing your 'before-after'.

There are two empty panels on the page overleaf. Use them to describe the 'before-after' for a particular customer or prospect that you are selling to.

Create The 'Before-After' For Your Solution

Before

After

Here are three tips to keep in mind as you set about creating a 'before-after':

Tip 1: Start by listing all the possible variables that you could present a 'before-after' for. Then select the top three to five based on what matters most to the customer and best differentiates your solution. Relate everything back to the buyer's needs and specifically to how the buyer will measure success or evaluate competing solutions.

Tip 2: Consider what you want the buyer to be thinking, saying and doing after seeing your 'before-after'. For example:

- **Thinking**: We want those results! It is possible for us to achieve the same!
- **Saying**: 'We really need to look at this more closely ...'
- **Doing**: Engaging in a conversation with the seller around how such results can be achieved.

The test then is whether 'before-after' gets the responses that you want from the buyer.

Tip 3: Don't worry if you are struggling to complete the 'before-after' but please don't leave it blank – it is too important. Why not copy the page and share it with others to get their views. You could even use it with your customer or prospect to get their views on their present needs and what they want to achieve by buying your IT solution.

Tee-Up Your 'Before-After'

As we see later, sellers are rightly cautious about presenting the buyer with a *fait accompli* set of numbers. They don't want to be seen to be producing numbers 'out of a hat' and generating buyer resistance as a result.

For this reason how the 'before-after' analysis is 'teed-up' is important. The following is the type of **pre-amble that works** well:

> *Here are some of the typical results achieved by our customers – it may be different for your business, but people find it a good starting point in terms of working out what results to expect.*

It sounds obvious, but it is also useful to ask the buyer in advance whether he or she would like to see some of the results that have been achieved by others, or to look at some numbers. This is often **a good test of where the buyer is at** and what exactly he or she is thinking.

Update Your Sales Vocabulary

Justifying the purchase of IT increasingly requires engaging with the senior managers who control budgets and set priorities. The opportunity or challenge for many salespeople is to sell higher. It is at this audience that the seller is aiming his 'before-after' and other aspect of the sales proposition.

The salesperson who wants to sell higher must speak the same language as the C-level executive who now makes, or shapes, decisions regarding what is spent and when. The salesperson must speak the language of the CEO, CFO, COO and so on.

Even if you are not quite selling to C-level, that is still the language that you need to use. Regardless of the level at which you are selling, this is **the language that gets projects and purchases approved** within large organizations.

Based on an analysis of hundreds of C-level conversations we put together a glossary of the language that salespeople must use to sell higher. To boost your success you need to pack your presentations, conversations and proposals with these terms:

Talking about direction...

Success
Strategy
Objectives
Vision
Goals
Business Drivers
Strategic Priorities
Strategic Agenda
Strategic Direction
Strategic Fit
Strategic Alternatives
Strategic Options

Talking about their industry...

Growth Rates
Market Share
Market Trends
Market Opportunities & Threats
Must Win Battles
Innovation
Cost Cutting
Improved Efficiency
Down-sizing /right-sizing
Doing More With Less
Out-sourcing and In-sourcing
Core competence

Talking about what matters...

Key Success Factors
KPIs
Risk / Dependencies & Milestones
Gaps
Benchmarking
Competitive Advantage
Compliance
Regulations / Standards

Talking about results....

Results
Performance
Business Case
Financials
Profit and Loss
Balance Sheet
Investment
Payback
Metrics / KPIs
Cost-Benefit Analysis
ROI APR
Total Cost of Ownership
Full Lifecycle Costs
Total Project Costs

Talking about buying...

Budget
Justification
Business Case
Sign-off / Approval
Stakeholders / Politics
Sponsor
Buying Team
Cross-functional
Synergy
Implementation

Making it happen...

Visibility, Measurability
& Control
Change (change management)
Compliance
Implementation
Project planning / management
Accountability
Value Management
Risk Management

Having scanned the above table, how many of these terms did you use in your last sales pitch, presentation, or proposal? Are you having conversations with buyers on these subjects? If you are not then you're not quite selling to the new business-led and more senior executive behind more of today's important buying decisions.

Are You Using Business Impact to Sell?

Before moving on to the next section let's take stock. To do this, here is a quick test to see if your sales proposition is focused on:

Selling technology benefits and features

OR

**Helping the buyer to justify the decision
by communicating business impact.**

To find out see how many of the following questions can you tick with 'yes' answers?

- Do you **quantify the benefits** by putting numbers on them?
- Do you provide a **before and after comparison** so that the buyer is in no doubt regarding the benefit of your solution will have?
- Do you communicate the **specific results** that your solution will help the buyer to achieve?
- Are the results you are promising credible and backed-up by customer stories and **third party validation**?
- Are you using the **key metrics** relevant to the various key stakeholders in the decision?

- Do you clearly demonstrate how your solution relates to the performance (**priorities and strategies**) of the buyer's business?

- Do you understand (and indeed shape) how the customer **defines** success for the purchase?

How many of the seven questions could you answer 'yes' to? Don't worry if the number was low — that merely suggests that there is a lot of potential to increase the power of your sales pitches and proposals. It means that the route to boosting your closing success is clear.

If you are not communicating business impact then the likelihood is that you are having the wrong conversations at the wrong levels with inevitable consequences for your sales success.

The seven factors in the checklist are an indicator of the power of your benefits message. More than that they measure just how good an argument you are able to make for the purchase of your solution. So make a list of those that you should be doing, but are not. Why not list them and put them down as actions against some of the deals you are progressing.

Getting the Tools You Need

Now that we have established the importance of business impact as benefits of interest to the business buyer of IT, let's examine some of the tools you are going to need in order to communicate business value, including:

- A very **powerful sales question** (or set of questions) (examined in the next chapter)

- A **sales calculator (Chapter 16)**

- A framework for communicating price in the context of the **buyer's Total Costs (Chapter 17)**
- A set of buyer-friendly **ROI Tools (Chapter 18)**.

If you want to be heard, communicate in the universal language of the business case. Forget about the traditional value proposition, benefits and features. Focus instead on the numbers, the impact the business results ...

15: The #1 IT Sales Question

www.SellingintheClouds.com

Introduction

There are as many sales questions as there are sales techniques. But not all questions have the same power in terms of engaging the customer or closing the sale. There is one question that is more powerful than all, yet it is missing from so many sales conversations. It is the question about what success means for the customer.

Questions Asked by Sellers

Books have been written full of questions for salespeople to ask, but too many questions are as bad as too few. Sales success is about **asking the right questions**.

The following are typical of the key questions for salespeople:

- What are your needs and requirements?
- Is there a budget allocated? Or questions on BANT (budget, authority, timing and need).
- How satisfied are you with your existing solution?
- What are you looking for in a new supplier?

And of course there is the trinity of questions around buying process, buying rationale and the buying team:

- How will the decision be made?
- Who will make and shape the decision?
- Why will the decision be made?

BUT, what is the #1 question for salespeople to ask? Is it one of the above questions, or could it be something else?

Which Question Is Best?

In our research we set about finding a question that was powerful, regardless of the sales situation or the customer's industry. We wanted a universally applicable question.

Moreover we wanted to find a question that must be asked regardless of the stage of the sales cycle that the customer is at – one that could be used early as well as late in the sale.

Indeed, we wanted a question that could be used by key account managers, as well as other sales people (and indeed buyers). It should be relevant to the initial customer contact as to closing the sale.

If that was not enough, we wanted a question that was going to help the seller to engage with more senior decision-makers and connect with the buyer's real underlying motivation or business drivers.

Most important of all, we wanted the question to help the salesperson to move the conversation off price and onto value. That of course is a 'tall order' in an age of buyer obsession with price and payback.

The #1 Question Revealed

We conducted much consultation, discussion and debate before we settled on what we felt was the #1 Sales Question.

The results might surprise some people. That is because in most of the sales conversations we have studied the question selected as the number one does not get asked regularly. Indeed, it is present in only the best of the best sales meetings, pitches and proposals. Here is the question:

What does success for you look like?

Here is why the question is important: the more you can link what you are selling to the customer's success the greater the likelihood of your own sales success. So, can you answer this question for your customers and prospects?

The Power of the #1 Question

It sounds like a straightforward question, but the wording is important. That is to say, it is a much more powerful way of asking 'what are you trying to achieve?' or 'can you tell me about your requirements'. Indeed, it is the ultimate 'why?' question in that it goes to the very core of what the buyer is trying to achieve.

The #1 question is aimed at establishing the buyer's definition of success. That is arguably the most important (but too often overlooked) aspect of the seller's needs analysis. After all the most fundamental need of any buyer is what they define as success.

Success may be measured by the buyer at the level of a function, project team department business unit or organization. But, it does not really matter at what level success is measured, it is how you connect your solution to success at all levels that matters most.

Salespeople often ask us 'What if the customer has the wrong definition of success or no definition at all?'. The customer may be struggling to define success. Perhaps the customer's expectations are too high or too low. Either way that is a great opportunity for the salesperson to add value in terms of helping the buyer to clarify success.

Engaging in the discussion around success is the highest form of consultative or solution selling. It is where the seller can leverage customer stories, third party reports and industry benchmarks to powerful effect.

How the Customer Measures Success

The seller who can shape the buyer's definition of success is in pole position when it comes to winning the sale. On the other hand the seller who does not know, or understand what the buyer really wants to achieve is at real disadvantage. The #1 question can be a real differentiator.

An important part of understanding what success means for the buyer is to understand how success will be measured. That is the metrics, KPIs and other variables that will be used to gauge success. So, after you ask the 'success' question, ask 'What business metrics or drivers will it impact on?'.

Linking to the Buyer's Success

As a sales person you obviously want to link your solution to the buyer's success. So the goal is to present the benefits of your solution in terms of the impact on the buyer's key metrics.

Asking the success question is not just about numbers and cold business logic. You want to connect with the buyer's vision for success. That is why the question asks 'what does success **look like for you**?'. It is aimed at helping the buyer to envision or visualize success at a personal, departmental and organizational level.

As a salesperson you want to connect your solution with the buyer's vision of success, even his or her hopes, aspirations and dreams. That makes the #1 question an exercise in creative visualization and motivation. It is positive and future-focused.

Engage around Success

Asking questions about success is a powerful way of getting the customer thinking. It has the potential to unlock a new level of engagement, because it is not the type of question that buyers expect to be asked regularly.

For the customer who is expecting a sales pitch, a genuine conversation about success is quite a pleasant surprise. When the salesperson gets the buyer thinking about success, it inevitably leads to a discussion on key success factors, as well as possible risks or barriers to success. This is fertile ground for the salesperson as these are hooks upon which the solution and benefits are hung.

Getting the Purchase Order

In an age where buying decisions are governed by approvals procedures and budgetary controls defining success can be key to getting the purchase order sanctioned.

Buyers must be in a position to justify their decisions and being able to explain the results achieved as a result of a purchase is key.

If the buyer cannot define success then perhaps the salesperson should be cautious about the likelihood of the decision being made, at least in the short-term.

Success for Different Stakeholders

The success question needs to be asked of all stakeholders because the definition of success can vary across a buying team / unit.

This is another place that the salesperson can add value in helping the buyer to reconcile the divergent needs of different stakeholders.

Your #1 Question

Do you ask the success question of your customers and prospects on a regular basis? By doing so you are sending a message to the customer that you care about and want to contribute to their success. That in itself is enough to distinguish you from others.

More important still you are opening up a deeper conversation with the buyer and matching your solution with the buyer's needs at the most fundamental level.

Think about how you can apply the success question across your sales cycle by reflecting on the following questions:

- How can you integrate stories of success into your lead generation materials?
- Do you ask your customers the success question when you first interact?
- Is defining success for the customer a key element of your needs analysis?
- Do you build your proposal around the customer's definition of success?
- Do you move the buyer from price to value by connecting your solution with their success?
- Do you check to ensure that success is achieved after the sale, as the basis for the next sale?

Are there items listed above that you should be doing, but are not? Why not list them and put them down as actions against some of the deals you are progressing.

16: The IT Sales Calculator

Introduction

Surprisingly one of the main challenges facing IT vendors is a mathematical one. That is because to win the sale, or to avoid being hammered on price, may require challenging how the buyer does their math.

Buyers' Obsession with Numbers

Buyers are increasingly numbers-obsessed. Vendors tend to be less so and would typically prefer to 'talk price' only after all the benefits have been presented. Indeed salespeople can be a little frustrated by buyers who:

- Interrupt the flow of their perfectly planned sales pitch to ask about price up front
- Immediately turn to the price page (often the last page) of the seller's proposal, paying little attention to what has come before it
- Have unrealistic expectations and want 'everything for nothing'.

But are buyers as in-tune with the numbers as their behavior would suggest? For most sellers the answer is 'no'.

In selling to the modern buyer you can't change the fact that they are obsessed with numbers, but you can influence the numbers that they are looking at. Most importantly you can draw their gaze from lowest price to best value.

The Math Challenge Facing Sellers

From the point of view of many IT vendors there is a problem with how buyers do their math. For example buyers often err in how they calculate the real or total cost of alternative IT products, or solution. But it is only half of the story.

Problems with how value is calculated are perhaps even more common than errors in calculating cost. Moreover they have worrying implications for the seller and often result in pressure on price.

The Math of Selling

Many of the challenges in selling to today's numbers-obsessed IT buyers are mathematical ones. To understand why this is the case let's look at the buyer's calculator.

You can see the problem, can't you? Yes, the calculator is missing several keys.

The Buyer's Broken Calculator

As far as many IT vendors are concerned, the only key actively used by today's buyers is the minus or subtract key – it is actively used in cutting vendor prices and margins. That is the math challenge at the core of selling.

The challenge for sellers is to improve the buyer's math and it starts with focusing the buyer on value, as opposed to just price. It requires getting the buyer do more multiplication and long division and less subtraction!

Results Require More than Subtraction

No IT manager's business equation is so simple that it can be calculated with just the minus or subtract key on a calculator. Results are not that easily got!

We all have made mistakes in our math when making a purchase decision that was narrowly focused on cost. Think for example of a situation where you bought what appeared to be the cheapest solution, only to find that it ended up being much more expensive than you had expected once the running costs or hidden extras were taken into account. Well, it happens surprisingly often even to professional buyers.

The risk of doing the math wrong is greatest where:

- The buyer is in a hurry
- There is real pressure to cut costs
- There is not enough attention paid to the long-term consequences of decisions
- The buyer is inexperienced or new.

The 'cheapest' IT solution or vendor is not always the best, at least not when the buyer does his or her math properly. If the buyer's calculator was working properly it might reveal that the cheapest solution would end up costing more in the long-term.

A blind obsession with price can result in basic business math being neglected, with only the minus key being used. But if subtraction is all that is going on, the buyer will lose sight of such metrics as return on investment or total cost of ownership.

The metrics increasingly used to build the business case for IT projects and purchases require some element of addition, multiplication and long division.

The challenge for the vendor is to fix the buyer's broken calculator – to give the buyer a better way of arriving at the numbers that he or she needs.

Math – A Shared Challenge

Buyers and sellers both have problems with numbers. More to the point they have problems in getting others to believe or accept their numbers. In respect of both buyer and seller this has the potential to impact on earnings.

Increasingly buyers want to see an ROI justification from sellers, yet they are slow to believe them when they get them. The reasons for doubting the seller's numbers are manifold.

Little do sellers realize that the buyer's own numbers are subject to similar skepticism from their own internal colleagues, most notably from the Finance department. Indeed figures suggest that **savings claimed by Procurement and business / project sponsors are typically discounted by up to 60%** when they are reviewed internally.

That last paragraph is worth reading twice. Sellers often say 'surely it is the seller's claims that will be discounted by procurement'. Yes that happens for sure, but the point we are making is that the buyer who strives so much to negotiate a price reduction from the seller is likely to have his claimed savings discounted too.

Math – The Credibility Challenge

The IT manager may face an up-hill struggle in getting others to accept his or her numbers. The biggest skeptics are often in Finance. They regularly throw cold water on savings claims.

In many organizations the professional buyer is only one (the first) gatekeeper and that there are often others even more skeptical lying in wait behind them.

There are many reasons why the buyer's savings claims are discounted. For example there may be a problem with the method of calculation, over-optimism, or the leakage of savings and other promised benefits during implementation. The result is that executives struggle to get their IT projects or purchases approved and that hinders them in doing their job.

Not only is it a cause of frustration among executives, it can also be detrimental to earnings. That is because one dollar in five earned by Procurement, for example, is linked to the achievement of results and paid in the form of a bonus (Institute of Supply Management Salary Survey 2011).

What does all this mean for the seller? Well it means that the seller's painful concessions made during the negotiation process may not be enough. The buyer may return for more concessions if the previous set of numbers has been discredited.

So it is that the buyer and the seller share the same goal – a highly credible business case / justification – one that can withstand the scrutiny of internal skeptics and even saboteurs.

You Need a Calculator to Negotiate

Although the buyer's calculator may be broken many sellers don't have a calculator at all. That is a real problem when sellers want to justify their price by for example:

- Demonstrating a lower total cost ownership
- Calculating the value of their solutions.

These so called 'math challenges' are no simple matter; it is advanced algebra so to speak. Take for example the challenge of calculating the payback from an investment in IT.

The ultimate test of your sales message, pitch or proposal is to encourage the buyer to take out a calculator or spreadsheet.

Sellers must encourage their buyers to use more and better math. They must provide their customers with a better calculator, spreadsheet and business case. Otherwise a compelling argument for the purchase of their solution cannot be demonstrated.

Improving the Buyer's Math

Could you sit down with an accountant (or accountant-type) for 30 minutes and absolutely convince him or her of the merits of your solution? That is a key measure of the type of skill required to sell to today's numbers-obsessed buyers.

Sellers require a new dexterity with numbers. That includes getting to grips with the wide range of acronyms that go along with it, including TCO, ROI, EBIT and so on. These are terms you will see explained in the **Appendix**.

Some sellers say 'I am never asked for those things', or that their customers are not that sophisticated. But that makes the seller's math more, rather than less, important.

If your customers are not doing the numbers on your proposition then that is a great opportunity. If they are doing the numbers and not involving you then that is a greater opportunity still. Either way you need to put the power of basic math to work in your selling.

*The business case is essential for the seller who wants to **move conversation off price and onto value**. That is a real challenge in terms of today's increasingly price-obsessed buyers'*

Lean Selling

The challenge around numbers for many buyers is to find ways to spend less. That is a reality that IT vendors need to grapple with. It can be summed up in the word 'lean' and rather than spending more it means:

- Doing more for less
- Making it go further
- Curtailing spending
- Slimming it down – cutting it back
- Driving out new efficiencies
- Extending its life – retiring it later
- Leveraging existing resources
- Doing it in-house
- Delaying it – stretching it out
- Renegotiating the price
- Driving a better deal
- Focusing on results and effectiveness
- Deliver maximum value for money.

So therein lies the challenge for sellers of IT in today's business environment – lean selling. That is selling IT solutions that help the buyer to spend less, rather than more. And when we do expect them to spend more it is to enable them to save even more still.

Helping The Buyer with the Numbers?

Most buyers face pressure in terms of their numbers. Rather than being a problem for the seller, it can be an opportunity. That is, if the seller can help the buyer with his or her numbers.

Can you help the buyer to generate numbers that are compelling enough to ensure that the purchase or the project gets internal approval and that it wins out over other competing projects or purchases?

To find out how you can help the buyer with his or her numbers ask yourself: can you help the buyer to:

- Work out the numbers?
- Identify what metrics to use?
- Track what is being spent and what is being saved with you?
- Benchmark his or her numbers against industry norms?
- Make the numbers more robust in the face of external scrutiny?
- Build a model or spreadsheet?
- Learn about the results achieved by others by providing customer case studies, or facilitating customer visits?
- Alleviate pressure on his or her numbers?
- Make his or her numbers bullet-proof?
- Claim credit and get rewarded for his or her numbers?

Are there items listed above that you should be doing, but are not? Why not list them and put them down as actions against some of the deals you are progressing.

17: The TCO Iceberg

Know Your Customer's TCO

When it comes to the customer's costs, your price may only be the tip of the iceberg. That is because the price may represent only a small proportion of the buyer's total costs. Although often overlooked, it has important implications for both buyer and seller.

The business case can be used to show the buyer that buying the cheapest solution may end up costing more in the long run, or that collaborating with the seller to lower the TCO can deliver a return many times that which can be achieved by shaving a few percentage points off the seller's margin.

The Iceberg Principle in Selling

The iceberg principle is a powerful metaphor for your customer's TCO. That is because, just like an iceberg, much of the bulk of the buyer's total costs in respect of any IT project or purchase are not obvious.

The reality is that in budgeting for any IT project there are costs that are often hidden. They can dwarf the purchase price when it comes to calculating total cost of ownership or total lifecycle costs.

The price of the vendor's hardware or software, although plain to see, may account for only a relatively small proportion of the customer's total cost. In the iceberg diagram shown overleaf up to 85% of the total customer's costs are hidden.

It is important that your customer has an accurate picture of the total cost of fixing their problem or addressing their need, as well as of the price of your solution.

When the iceberg looks like that shown in the diagram the 'cheapest solution' often turns out to be the 'dearest'. Buying a cheaper solution is a false victory, unless it improves the total cost equation.

Buyer and seller need to clearly understand the total cost of acquiring, storing, using, maintaining and even decommissioning or replacing across the total lifecycle of the product. They need to know the iceberg.

Price Really Isn't Everything!

Today's buyers are increasingly obsessed with price. However, most salespeople can justifiably argue that when it comes to buying their solution 'price isn't everything!'.

A supplier price renegotiation may only be a false victory for the buyer, where the purchase price accounts for only a small proportion of the buyer's total cost. While negotiating hard on your price the buyer may be missing out on the real source of savings.

The message for the buyer is 'look out for the iceberg!'. But, this is an important message for sellers also. Some salespeople are every bit as obsessed about price as the buyers they sell to.

The result is that they can be drawn into price negotiation before they have communicated the value of what they are selling.

Icebergs Can Be Dangerous!

Selling to a customer who has only a surface level appreciation of the TCO puts your margin and perhaps even the deal at risk.

Indeed, miscalculating the TCO can have 'Titanic' consequences for both the seller and the buyer:

- The buyer who does not spot the iceberg is at risk of an unpleasant surprise. He or she has clearly not got their numbers in order and sooner or later somebody is likely to draw attention to it. This may call the very viability of the decision into question, or cause the purchase to stall

- If the seller is unaware of the total iceberg in terms of costs then he or she is disadvantaged in terms of negotiating and will struggle to move the conversation off price and onto value. Helping the buyer to see the value requires that the customer understands their total cost.

The seller who can enlighten the customer regarding the iceberg principle can uncover new ways to deliver value for the buyer, while at the same time protecting margins. That makes the TCO Iceberg a key tool for value-based selling.

Draw Your Customer's TCO Iceberg

Draw the iceberg for your customer – showing the cost price of your solution above the water and the rest of the customer's other costs below the water. Such costs might include:

- Internal time and resources
- Overheads
- Expenses
- Opportunity cost
- Hidden fees and charges.

These can exist under headings, such as:

- Buying (sourcing, selecting, contracting, procurement, etc.)
- Warehousing, packaging and logistics costs
- Customization
- Quality control
- Implementation
- Switching costs
- Training and support
- Ongoing licenses
- Maintenance
- Energy and other operating costs.

The list of possible costs that make up TCO is endless – so it is important to **determine the specific costs for your customer** and how they are measured.

When you have your iceberg created help melt your customer's iceberg, starting from the bottom up.

Where Savings Really Can Be Made!

The supplier's price, while it is the most obvious place to look for savings, is rarely the most profitable. This can be seen in the table:

		Your Price As a % of TCO				
		5%	10%	15%	20%	30%
% Saving Achieved	5%	0.3%	0.5%	0.8%	1.0%	1.5%
	10%	0.5%	1.0%	**1.5%**	2.0%	3.0%
	15%	0.8%	1.5%	2.3%	3.0%	4.5%
	20%	1.0%	2.0%	3.0%	4.0%	6.0%
	25%	1.3%	2.5%	3.8%	5.0%	7.5%
	30%	1.5%	3.0%	4.5%	6.0%	9.0%
	35%	1.8%	3.5%	**5.3%**	7.0%	10.5%
	40%	2.0%	4.0%	6.0%	8.0%	12.0%

For example, a saving of 10% (left hand column) on a purchase price that amounts to only 15% of the total cost (top row), results in only a saving 1.5% overall.

Indeed on the same basis saving just 5% of the overall total costs would require a massive 35% cut in supplier price.

The lesson is an obvious one – buyers are often focused on getting savings in the wrong areas. Sellers must help the buyer to cut the TCO.

Use the table shown earlier to calculate the relative scope for savings for the buyer based on the proportion of total costs accounted for by your solution. Then tell the buyer that you can help him or her save lots of money in a variety of ways if you work together.

Educate the buyer to the fact that the savings that can be achieved by working together dwarf what can be achieved simply by a supplier price cut. To do this convincingly you will need to know your TCO iceberg.

Draw Your TCO Iceberg

What proportion of the customer's TCO or total lifecycle cost is accounted for by your solution? Find out by listing all the costs associated with the acquisition, implementation and indeed all stages of the lifecycle of your product in your customer's hands. Add up the TCO and the customer's total project cost.

Draw the iceberg for your customer – showing the cost price of your solution above the water and the rest of the customer's other costs below the water. Create an iceberg diagram (like the one on the next page) to highlight your impact on the customer's total costs.

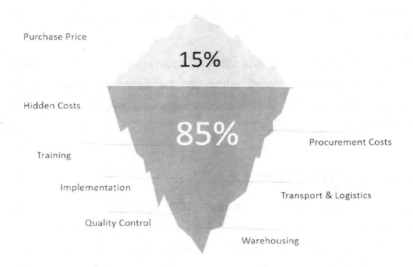

Let's look at a great example of how you can use the TCO iceberg to help you to sell. It is aimed at giving you the inspiration you need.

An Inspirational TCO Iceberg

The Swiss industrial fastener supplier Bossard (**www.bossard.com**) uses the iceberg model to powerful effect. They call it 'The Rule of 15-85' in respect of the TCO model in fastening:

Here is how they explain it on their website:

> *On average, the fastener itself makes up to only around 15% of the total costs. The remaining 85% of the costs come from development, procurement, testing, inventories, assembly and logistics. This chain of events is adding costs to the entire fastening ecosystem. Experience in the industry has shown that cost savings of 50% and*

more can be achieved in the areas of logistics and engineering. This has a lasting effect on the total costs of the end product.

How does this fit into the company's sales proposition? Again quoting the company's website:

At Bossard, every solution we create, is designed to reduce costs, according to the TCO concept in fastening.

Why not use this last sentence but replace the name 'Bossard' and the product 'fastening' with your company's name and product, or service below.

At ...., every solution we create, is designed to reduce costs, according to the TCO concept in ....

Then take it one step further and list the top three ways in which you reduce your customers' TCO:

1. _____

2. _____

3. _____

Slippery Icebergs in IT

Calculating the TCO can be difficult. Here are just some of the challenges you may encounter:

- Different aspects of the TCO may come out of different budgets and accounting periods
- Many of the costs may be discounted as 'soft' rather than 'hard' savings by those who apply accounting principles
- Many are fixed costs and that makes them difficult to reduce, for example wages and salaries
- Calculating TCO involves forecasts, assumptions and scenarios.

Add to these factors the fact that the seller may only have limited access to the information from the buyer. However, it is precisely because it is difficult that it is all the more worthwhile.

Your competitors won't have embraced the TCO concept precisely because it is difficult. That means if you wrestle with it you will be rewarded. However, it does not mean that you need an encyclopedic knowledge of the customer's costs and other numbers. As we will see in the next chapter there are advantages to avoiding too much detail, particularly at the start.

18: ROI IT Sales Tools

Introduction

Too many ROI tools don't survive contact with the buyer. The problem is two-fold – it relates to the tools themselves, as well as to how they are used. This is compounded by the fact that sellers can be quick to put their numbers aside at the appearance of any resistance by the buyer.

What many sellers don't realize is that there is no perfect set of numbers and that the process of engaging with buyers in the challenge of calculating the ROI on IT is what matters most.

Having a 'down to earth' discussion around the ROI for IT in the clouds, or elsewhere, is essential to selling to the business buyer. The principles of such an approach are presented in this section.

10 Reasons Buyers Don't Believe Your ROI

Yes, everybody wants it, but nobody believes it! It's not a cryptic clue – we are talking about **ROI**.

Buyers want to see the seller's ROI model (and will be very suspicious if you don't have one). Yet in most cases they don't believe them once they are provided.

We have listened to buyers on the subject of the ROI models provided by salespeople. Using their own words, we have compiled the top 10 reasons ROI models are greeted with cynicism:

- **We have our own** – 'we prefer to use our own model' – 'salespeople only use a model to give them ammunition to sell'

- **Our business is different** – 'that model is more suited to other companies ... in other sectors ... of a different size ... '

- **It is too complex** – 'there are too many sheets, too many calculations, too many assumptions, etc'

- **It is too simplistic** – 'in theory and on paper that is fine, but in reality it is more difficult to arrive at a figure ...' or 'Finance would dismiss those numbers out of hand on the basis that they are an over-simplification'

- **It is subjective** – 'what else would you say (being a salesman)!'

- **It doesn't consider the total cost of ownership** –'OK, you put the cost at 1.5 million, but that is just your charges, there will be a lot more cost on our side'

- **The assumptions made are not verified** – for example 'the efficiency gain you have put at 50%, but what is that based on? Is that backed up by research, or by your customers?'

- **It is presented as a *fait accompli*** – 'if we are not involved in creating the model, then we don't own it'

- **You can't put numbers on it** – 'building a business case is a good idea, but it is not really going to work'

- **It is confidential** – sellers often have 'to pull numbers out of a hat' because buyers say they cannot share the information that would prevent seller guesswork.

With these obstacles in mind let's examine how ROI models can be made more effective.

Surviving an Attack on Your ROI

When a buyer claims that the numbers are not relevant, inaccurate or unrepresentative that is a real test of the seller's confidence. And it is a test that many fail, when they:

- Hurriedly put the numbers aside and disengage with the issue of economics altogether
- Dismiss the buyer's contention with a retort, such as 'these are the numbers that others use' or 'that is the first time that I have heard questions around the model'.

Sometimes the buyer is testing the seller for his or her reaction by saying 'I don't believe those numbers'. The buyer is throwing down the gauntlet so to speak.

Rather than putting the numbers aside it is important for the seller to respond in a calm, confident and engaging manner. For example by saying 'sure, which numbers in particular would you adjust?'. And asking 'what figures do you think would more closely represent your business?'.

Why ROI Kick-back Is Welcome

Getting kick-back from your prospect regarding your ROI is not necessarily a bad thing. It is worse if your prospect sits there and says nothing. Any reaction to your ROI is better than no reaction. It shows that the buyer is engaged.

It is better that the buyer says 'I don't believe those numbers' than that they nod politely and let the seller leave thinking that his or her numbers have been accepted. If the seller knows that there are doubts about the numbers then he or she can discuss and work to resolve them.

So next time the buyer raises questions about your numbers don't say 'duh oh!', say 'great' – the buyer is engaged – now we can really get the conversation going.

Engaging the Buyer with Your ROI

Here are some of the strategies to engage customers more effectively around your ROI:

- It is important for the seller to **ask the buyer whether he or she is interested in seeing an ROI model** and to gauge that it is being presented to the right person or at the right time. If a discussion around the ROI is unwelcome for the buyer (for whatever reason) he or she is going to take a pot shot at the seller's model

- It is important to **'tee up' the model correctly** to explain its role and to state any limitations up front. For example:

    This is a model which has been developed over the course of the past three years and some 25 installations ...

    ... its purpose is not to present you with an iron-clad ROI for your business but to demonstrate what such a model might look like, including some of the key variables and factors to be considered.

    ... It is a generic model and would need to be tailored to the specifics of your business, but other customers have found it useful in getting an initial high level view of the payback ...

- An attack on your numbers may be as much about the buyer **struggling with how to build the business case**, as it is about your ROI tool. Calculating the ROI for IT and getting agreement around any set of numbers is difficult. Indeed, it is likely to frustrate the buyer. But just because something is difficult does not mean that the seller should shy away from it. On the contrary helping the buyer to wrestle with the numbers may be an important differentiator and a powerful source of influence.

- The seller should not feel under pressure to **have all the answers** when it comes to the buyer's numbers. It is perfectly acceptable to answer 'I don't know', or 'it depends' when asked a question about payback or metrics. That is of course as long as it is followed by saying something like 'I would be delighted to share with you some of the metrics used by others, or to help you calculate some numbers for your business'.

- When it comes to the ROI the **process of arriving at the number** is as important as the number itself. The buyer cannot realistically expect the seller to present the perfect ROI model without engagement – it has to be developed jointly. The seller should acknowledge that building an ROI **presents challenges** and offer their ROI model in that context. What they are effectively saying is 'here is one way of trying to put numbers on this ...'.

- It is important to remember that the burden of proof remains with the salesperson in respect of justifying why any particular ROI information is being presented by the vendor. This is where **external validation** is particularly important in explaining how the model was derived, how key assumptions were made and so on.

Why Many ROI Tools Don't Get Used

In many organizations we have witnessed a surprising trend where expensive newly-developed ROI tools are not being used. Here is what happens: marketing spearheads the development of a set of ROI tools. When they are ready they are put on the intranet for the sales staff to access and even on the Internet for customers to use directly. There they sit – waiting to be used.

The problem is typically not that salespeople do not know that the tools exist. It is that they are slow to use them. We hear comments such as:

- 'It is too detailed and not easy to use ...'
- 'I am not comfortable using it ...'
- 'We have not received any training on it ...'
- 'It raises more questions than it answers ...'
- 'If I get asked a question on it I don't think I would be able to answer it ...'
- 'It can take the conversation in a direction I am not comfortable with ....'
- 'Buyers don't believe our numbers ...'
- 'You need to take out the laptop, or go online to use it ...'
- 'We give it to the customer and let them use it themselves (if they want to) ...'.

Clearly creating an ROI tool is not enough. Creating ROI tools that are widely used by the sales team requires more.

The lesson is clear – you cannot simply hand the salesperson an ROI tool – he or she must be guided in how to use it.

So They Don't Need an ROI!

Some salespeople tell us that they don't need an ROI, or are not asked for one by their prospects. We get worried when we are told:

- 'The buyer is not interested ...'
- 'They do not ask to see it ...'
- 'For engineers the ROI is not the key factor ...'.

If salespeople are not being asked for an ROI then they may not be selling to enough business (as opposed to technical) managers and in particular to sufficiently senior managers. We truly believe that those salespeople who are not using an ROI face a greater risk of lost or stalled deals.

Those who sell to technical buyers are more focused on features than financials. This is a risk because of the continued shift in decision-making power from technical staff to Procurement, Finance and others.

Not using an ROI is a major lost opportunity for the IT vendor. That is because even technical decisions need to be justified in business terms, including a cost / benefits analysis or ROI. Just because the salesperson is not being asked for an ROI does not mean that one is not needed. Rather the issue may be that buyer does not feel that the seller should be involved in the numbers debate.

Develop Your ROI Credibility

The **process by which buyers are engaged** around numbers and how any ROI tool is used is every bit as important (if not more important) than the tool itself. Remember, presenting the buyer with a set of numbers is not the objective – rather it is to engage the buyer in a conversation regarding the ROI or payback.

How can your ROI tool(s) be improved? Can they be made easier to use, visually more engaging for the buyer, or tailored in terms of level of detail to the stage of the sale? Can they be customized to reflect different industries and their own unique language?

While many ROI tools are clumsy and in need of improvement, it is important to point out that it is not about **the perfect ROI model.**

There is a real danger of making ROI calculators that are too sophisticated or smart.

What is required is an easy to use and credible tool that engages the buyer in exploring the key benefits of your solution. In fact it is probably a series of models or tools. This is important, as the first introduction to the concept of payback or financial return from your solution is likely to be at a high level, perhaps using standard industry figures, or benchmarks and based on the results typically achieved by other customers.

As the sales cycle progresses the seller hopefully will get a chance to get into more detail and will be involved in **building a business case** that is tailored to the specifics of the customer's business. However, the business case should always be communicated right from the initial sales meetings and presentations, using examples and averages based on other clients.

Salespeople need an easy to use and credible tool to calculate ROI and other key metrics that will help buyers explore the impact the solution will have on their business. However, they also need customer case studies, references, white papers and industry data to back up the figures they provide.

Using Scenarios to Sell

Predicting the future is not easy, and that is exactly what the ROI tries to do. But today's perfect plan could be completely invalidated by a change in the competitive situation, an upset in the market or any one of a host of other factors outside the company's control.

There are three key reasons why ROI projections get it wrong. You can think of them as the 'Three Temptations'. They are the temptation to:

- Underestimate cost
- Exaggerate benefits
- Underestimate the time required.

Most business cases fall victim to at least one of these problems. For example, in the area of IT projects it is regularly documented that 80% of projects fail.

The salesperson can usefully embrace the uncertainty around precise numbers. That involves doing some sensitivity analysis in respect of the three key variables (as well as others). Thus a key question for discussion between buyer and seller is: 'What would be the impact of a 5%, 10% or 15% variance in terms of the benefits, costs, or timing?'.

19: Selling To 'The Mess'

Introduction

With so much talk of the business case you would think that buying IT was a purely logical affair. The reality however is much different.

Buying can be messy, but success for the seller depends on how he or she can cope with increased complexity and constant change.

Why Buying Can Be Messy

We all know that buying can be messy. Buyers don't always know exactly what they want and even if they do, they may struggle to get their colleagues to agree. The menu of complicating ('messiness') factors, includes:

- Missing information
- Conflicting requirements
- Competing projects
- Shifting priorities
- Changing requirements
- Diverse stakeholders
- Political tensions
- Changing strategies
- Emerging technologies
- Changing market conditions
- Mergers and acquisitions
- Slashed budgets
- Compliance requirements.

Add to the list of 'messiness factors' the requirements of internal procurement processes and procedures and selling to large organizations is certainly not straightforward.

How messy is your sale? Check how many of the 13 'messiness factors' above apply!

Every one of the messiness factors listed above has the potential to stall a deal. **A key question is 'How much of the mess needs to be cleaned up before you can close the deal?'.**

While the mess can stall a sale, removing it has the potential to accelerate or unlock it. So how the seller deals with the mess is very important.

Why the Mess Matters

The messiness of the IT decision typically increases with the length of the time required to decide, the number of stakeholders involved, the level of novelty of the decision, the perceived level of risk and so on.

Messiness generally drives up the cost of the sale, lengthens the sales cycle and makes it all more unpredictable in terms of forecasting the deal. Not only can it often make the customer messy to sell to, but it can also make service and support a challenge.

The mess creates opportunities, as well as challenges. Sometimes there is money in the mess, other times there is just mess. If unmanaged it can cost the seller money, in other cases the seller may be rewarded, or even paid, for sorting the mess. A key question is: 'is there messy stuff that can help you win the sale?'.

Selling Amid the Mess

How can the seller take control of this mess, or should they even try? We suggest that salespeople, like all others in business, should seek to embrace, rather than control, the mess.

The level of mess is an important part of the pre-qualification of any opportunity. Sometimes the mess is a problem, and not an opportunity. The salesperson cannot advance the deal because:

- The confusion, ambiguity and lack of clarity is too profound
- All the people involved may not be able to agree
- It may not be possible to accommodate all the conflicting requirements
- The timing may simply not be right.

As a general principle the seller should engage with the mess. However, there will be cases where the salesperson may need to go away and come back when some of the mess has sorted itself out.

Where Is the Mess?

Where is the chaos, the confusion and the mess? Is it around the strategy, the solution, or the supplier? Is the mess related to the economics, risk, strategy, compliance or politics? Pin-pointing where the challenges are is important to enable the salesperson to be effective.

The mess can be greatest at **the early stages** of a complex buying decision, when everything is 'up in the air' and there are lots of questions to be answered. Here the objective of the seller is to help the buyer to set out the questions that need to be answered and to set out a process for the same.

The mess becomes a real problem where the **purpose, roles and responsibilities** are not clear. That is because a compelling 'why' creates the motivation and the momentum to cut through a lot of the 'how?' questions.

If there is a lack of clarity regarding scope, strategy and the vision of success, then this is where the salesperson should focus. If the objectives or benefits are compelling enough then that can break through any amount of mess. Of particular importance is helping the buyer to define what success is – it can have tremendous power. This is examined in detail in **Chapter 15**.

The most obvious of the messiness factors is **missing information**. This can take a variety of forms, including a deficit in information, understanding, or experience. This may result in the buyer over-complicating or over-simplifying the decision.

While **information gaps** can be relatively easy to fill, it can be more difficult to tackle false assumptions, misconceptions, or blind spots. All of these can amount to alternate views of reality in respect of the project or purchase – why it is needed and what it will achieve.

Change can be particularly messy, yet it is inherent in most IT projects and purchases. There is the people dimension – the challenge of changing behaviors, or gaining adoption. There is also the issue of politics and competing priorities or agendas. But changes are also required to ensure a fit with existing process, systems and structures. This makes careful planning and engagement with all those involved in any transition very important.

Should You Look to Find the Mess?

Experienced salespeople know that there is always some aspect of the buying decision that is going to be messy. So, if you cannot see any mess, then maybe you need to look a little closer.

For some sellers the more structured approach increasingly prevalent in buying is a comfort. **The buying process provides a degree of predictability** around what exactly the buyer is going to do next. However, as our research shows, the square boxes and straight lines of the buyer's process don't tell the full picture.

There is often an element of messiness even in the most rigid buying process. Beneath the veneer of the ordered and structured buying decision, or behind the facade of the confident and in-control buyer, lies the messy stuff.

The degree to which the salesperson can see and appreciate the messy elements of the buying decision is a measure of the degree of interaction, engagement and even empathy between the buyer and seller.

Getting Messy with Stakeholders

The process of stakeholder engagement and collaboration is key to revealing and managing any potential messiness factors that could impact on the sale. If you are not **hearing about the mess** – then you are probably not talking to the right people.

Buyers can be reluctant to confess internal dissention, missing information, crises of confidence and so on. It is a measure of their trust in the salesperson when they are willing to discuss and share these factors. However, bringing these issues out into the open is key to the success of any IT project.

There is a context to every project and purchase that **the salesperson cannot see**. That includes the culture of the organization, pressure on targets, style of leadership and the legacy of past projects.

Understanding the history of an organization is important to understand how messy a decision is likely to be. For this reason it is important for the salesperson to ask such questions as:

- Has a project or a decision been done / made like this before?
- If 'yes' what happened? If 'no' why not?

As a sales person should you tell the buyer that he's in a mess? Well, it is important to strike a balance between:

- Simplifying the decision for the buyer and perhaps in the process trying to sweep some of the mess under the carpet
- Complicating the decision, by drawing attention to any of the messiness.

But finding the right balance is not easy. On the one hand the seller may worry that a strategy of drawing attention to the mess may rebound by delaying the decision, or alienating the buyer who might believe that 'ignorance is bliss'.

For this reason it is important to test the buyer's awareness of, or sensitivity to, the messiness, while at the same time taking care not to scare him or her. The salesperson will then be heard asking questions such as:

- How satisfied are you that you are ready to make a decision?
- Is there a compelling reason to act at this time?
- Are you happy that all factors have been considered?
- Are there any issues that you feel need to be resolved?
- Are there any unaddressed risks or concerns?

- Are there any dissenting voices, or whispers?
- What is the level of comfort regarding a decision?
- Is the decision an easy one for the organization to make at this time?

Salespeople generally find that any bliss associated with ignorance is often short-lived. If the complicating factors are not acknowledged and dealt with early, they are likely to surface later – often with unforeseen consequences. The competing supplier who brings a previously unspoken or unseen risk factor into the buying decision – and solves it for the customer – can 'steal a march' on your company.

As a salesperson do you use the mess to sell – to heighten buyer sensitivity? Sellers who wish to draw buyer attention to messiness factors are often heard making statements, such as:

- 'It is an important decision and there are many factors to consider …'
- 'There are a number of possible scenarios …'
- 'Your business is different, you will have some specific requirements …'
- 'A fact-based analysis is an important first step in the process … Let's gather some information…'
- 'There are a number of steps that can be followed to systematically arrive at the right decision …'
- 'There are risks to consider and to manage …'
- 'It is important to allow sufficient time for analysis and planning … particularly to engage with the various stakeholders'

- 'This can be a complex area, it is important to plan it carefully ...'
- 'There is no magic bullet, or instant fix for this problem ...'
- 'More information is likely to be required before being able to make a decision ...'
- 'It is important to engage with the various stakeholders in order to ensure their ownership and buy-in ...'

Sometimes the decision is messy, but other times it is just the organization that's messy. So, it is important for the salesperson to understand the decision-maker's style and the organization's character before considering the impact of any messiness on the sale.

For example some companies are process-driven, they embrace structure and organization. Others are the opposite. They are unstructured and embrace informality. Most are somewhere between the two points on the continuum. This determines the degree of tolerance of messiness.

Taking Time to Uncover the Mess

The advice for salespeople is to take time to get comfortable with the mess. This has implications for the speed at which salespeople pitch their solutions.

Salespeople often feel under pressure to solve the customer's problem – that is before they have had an opportunity to discover exactly what the problem is, let alone to understand all of its nuances.

The sales fact-find can easily paint the requirements as black and white, so too can the buyer's RFP. But there is always messy stuff, even if people want to sweep it under the carpet. So, **what is the messy stuff that your prospect is struggling to deal with?**

When the buyer says 'tell me why we should buy your solution' the salesperson is tempted to recite their well-rehearsed sales script. They want to take control and tell the buyer what he or she should buy and why. After all, their company and its solutions provides the best solution and the right choice, regardless of any of the messy stuff.

However, salespeople who are less definitive, are less likely to be wrong. Those who take time to explore and experiment their way to the ideal solution for the buyer are less likely to be wrong too. That means getting in among the mess and being comfortable there. So the question for you is: **How comfortable are you with uncertainty, missing information and changing requirements?**

To help you say 'yes to mess' here are some points to bear in mind when you are closing a messy sale:

- We are not dealing with an ideal world – there is no point in idealizing the solution - slow down before presenting one – remember, as the Spanish proverb says 'it is much different to talk about bulls, than to be in the bullring'

- We are not starting with a blank canvas – when it comes to the complex sale there is a legacy of past decisions and present politics, as well as a requirement that what is bought must fit with the organization's culture, structures and systems

- There will be inevitable trade-offs and compromises within the buying organization – it is best to recognize them up front. For example, inevitably buyers want all the features of the premium solution, but only want to pay budget prices. A key part of the salesperson's job is to help the buyer to make the right trade-offs

- There is no such thing as perfect information – even if the information is available it can quickly go out of date; even if the information is completely objective the interpretation of it is not, there will always be gaps and blind spots

- In this information-pervasive age, the challenge for the salesperson is not to dump more information on the buyer, but to help the buyer in the evaluation, assimilation and interpretation of the right information (and by the way that is not the seller's marketing material)

- Everybody does not have to agree on everything and creative tension can be welcome. Indeed, if everybody agrees then moving beyond the *status quo* is going to be difficult. Diversity of opinions can be a good thing, indeed it is an important ingredient of progress and innovation. So the salesperson's job is to help the buyer to manage the process of arriving at a solution. That means combining the linear thinking of a scientist, or engineer, with the creative skills of an ad agency director

- Predicting the future is not easy, but where is no doubt, there is no opportunity. As Jim Collins, author of **Good To Great**, says 'chaos and confusion are necessary precedents to breaking through to new levels of performance'.

It is important for the buyer and seller to accommodate a certain amount of uncertainty. The secret is to focus not on having all the right answers, but in following a process that will arrive at the right answers.

20: Selling to the Hidden Agenda

sell to
hidden agenda

$ € ¥ £
$ € ¥ £
$ € ¥ £

www.SellingintheClouds.com

Introduction

We often think of the business manager as the epitome of logic and analysis. Obsessed with numbers and results, there is little time for emotion! But is that really true – what other than the business case shapes the decision?

It's Not Just Logic and Analysis!

Think of any famous business figure, or entrepreneur. Whether it is Bill Gates or Richard Branson, they are driven by **power, ambition, confidence and vision**. These are some of the most powerful emotions that there are!

Emotion is at the heart of what drives great managers and their businesses. Tapping into **what the buyer is feeling, as well as thinking** is therefore very important for the seller. However the traditional focus of needs analysis and fact-finds mean that it does not happen often enough. So the question is 'What is the role of emotion in the buying decision of your customers?'.

What Is the Emotional Agenda?

There is an emotional agenda to many buying decisions and in particular important, complex, or risky ones. The important question is 'How well does your sales pitch or proposal address this vital emotional agenda?'.

We often use the phrase '**justify with numbers – compel with emotion**'. That is because the emotional drivers of the buying decision:

- Are a powerful influence over behavior
- May not be purely rational

- Often go unexpressed and may even be subconscious
- Are inextricably bound up with our core attitudes, beliefs and values as well as our hopes and fears
- Are strongly influenced by others – they have a powerful socio-political dimension
- Act as the filters of perception thereby shaping our view of reality and our interpretation of events.

All these factors **make the emotional agenda of prime importance to the salesperson**. However identifying them can be a challenge.

Is There a Hidden Agenda?

Buyers rarely wear their emotions on their sleeves. Powerful though the emotions are, they may not be expressed and indeed can be subconscious. They are in the words of Kevin Allen, author of **The Hidden Agenda**:

> *Tapping into the buyer's hidden emotional agenda is the ultimate sales strategy. The ad man who coined the 'hidden agenda' phrase argues that it is **more important than the quality of the sales pitch or sales proposal and he is right!***

Increasingly sellers are beginning to realize that **success goes to the seller who can connect** with the buyer's hidden agenda.

Connecting with the Hidden Agenda

Connecting with the buyer's hidden agenda means that the salesperson strives to act as:

- A champion of the customers' values and ideals
- An ambassador for their vision and mission
- A counselor in respect of their fears

- A bulwark in terms of their risks and vulnerabilities.

Finding the Hidden Agenda – A Test for You

Go beyond stated requirements to uncover the hidden agenda – the fundamental underlying motives of the buyer. **Really get to know the buyer and what makes him or her think.**

Put It to Work

Here is a test of whether you understand your customer's hidden agenda. How many of the following questions can you answer (and relate your product, or solution to):

- What is it that matters most to them?
- What is it that fuels the buyer and his or her business or project?
- What keeps the buyer awake at night?
- What gets the buyer out of bed in the morning?
- What is the buyer's greatest hope / greatest frustration?
- What is his or her source of greatest pride?
- How do they imagine their future?
- What is the buyer's soft underbelly in terms of sensitivity, embarrassment, defensiveness and ego?
- Who do they admire aspire to be, or dread becoming?
- What are their core values?

So, how many of the above could you answer? Discovering the buyer's hidden emotional agenda is often a work in progress – it requires continual effort.

Bounded Rationality

This is the age of the utilitarian or economic buyer and the cost / benefits analysis, where IT decisions are made by weighing up the alternatives to determine the best outcome or deal. It is all very rational – or is it?

Have you ever heard a customer or prospect saying something like the following before deciding to buy:

- 'It feels right ...'
- 'There is a good fit ...'
- 'It all adds up ...'
- 'The time is right ...'
- 'It makes sense ...'
- 'I trust what the seller is saying ...'
- 'I can see it working ...'.

Are such statements based on rational argument or are they based on a more intuitive feeling? Well, often times it is both.

Yet confronted by increasingly hard-nosed buyers we can be tempted to overlook the role of buyer attitudes and instincts and get straight down to the cost / benefits analysis. That means we risk overlooking key buyer motivations and thus do not maximize our emotional leverage on the sale.

The Illusion of the 100% Analytical Buyer

Just as few buyers have pointed ears (like Mr Spock), few are entirely logical in their decision-making.

Although many IT buyers would like to deny it, their decisions are rarely 100% rational or analytical. Indeed, bounded rationality is the term used by scientists to describe the real complexity of human decision-making.

The Foibles of Human Buying Decisions

IT buying decisions are made by people not computers (although procurement systems are increasingly playing a role). That means, like any other decisions, buying decisions are subject to the foibles of human decision-making.

So, while most managers would scoff at the suggestion that he or she was in any swayed by emotion, it is a simple matter of brain chemistry that thinking cannot be divorced from feeling.

How Attitudes and Beliefs Shape Decisions

Our brains are hard-wired for emotion. Indeed those areas of the brain concerned with emotion pre-date the thinking parts of the brain by thousands of years. Quite simply that means that your buyer's decisions are not entirely analytical or rational. For example:

- A buyer's attitudes and beliefs will influence the information sources that we chose and then how we interpret that information. They are the filters of perception acting as a barrier to information or ideas that are incompatible with existing attitudes or beliefs

- A buyer's attitudes and beliefs also mean that he or she will sometimes take the easy route and skip the fact-gathering altogether. The buyer may prefer to work from what feels right, or on assumptions based on past experiences, many of which may be sub-conscious.

In the background, outside of the buyer's consciousness, the buyer will arrive at a split second instinct as to whether he or she trusts a sales person, or whether a particular situation 'feels right'.

These are just some of the ways in which IT buying decisions can fall short of being 100% rational or analytical. They explain why the term 'bounded rationality' describes buying as well as other forms of human decision-making.

Bounded Rationality in Buying

It is not a question of whether IT buying decisions are 100% rational or analytical, but whether they are 90%, 95% or 99% rational / analytical and 1%, 5% or 10% emotional, intuitive, or impulsive. That is bounded rationality.

Salespeople know only too well that it can be difficult to change a buyer's fundamental beliefs. They also know that even in the analysis of facts there is interpretation on the part of the buyer. That is bounded rationality too.

It Has to Feel Right for the Buyer

Confident IT buying decisions must intuitively feel right for the buyer. It is not enough that the cost / benefits analysis throws out the right number and that all the information has been gathered and evaluated thoroughly. Unless it 'feels right' a confident decision won't materialize and the buyer is at risk of prevarication.

The buyer may not be able to explain or rationalize it fully – it is not because all the information is not in, or there is a gap in the logic, but because quite simply 'it does not feel right'. Even though the analysis says 'yes', the buyer's instinct or intuition says 'no'.

Salespeople know that risk and politics, for example, introduce an element of uncertainty and complexity into the sale. It is no coincidence that these variables are heavily informed by intuition, instinct and feeling.

A political consideration will rarely be mapped in a spreadsheet, yet it may be intuitively inputted to the decision with all the 'what ifs'. The buyer may not have completed a risk register or computed numbers regarding probabilities of various risk, yet instinctively risk will enter the equation.

This has implications for selling – it is not just about the spreadsheet, the cost / benefits analysis or the business rationale for buying. The best way to handle an instinctive or emotive variable in the decision is not necessarily with more detailed information or more thorough analysis. That is important; however it goes deeper than that. The salesperson must address both the emotional and the logical elements of the purchase.

Appendix: The IT Sales Quiz

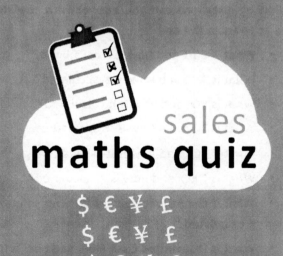

www.SellingintheClouds.com

Introduction

Your sales math can be a competitive differentiator. In particular it is key to price negotiations, protecting margins and moving the conversation off price and onto value.

This section contains a short Sales Math's Quiz. You can use it to pinpoint aspects that you can improve on, with the answers to the quiz forming a 'crash-course' on using a calculator to sell.

Check Your Math

Below you will find a simple test of your sales math. Now, it may seem like an innocent test, but don't be fooled. If you cannot answer some of these questions you could be missing out on what could be a very persuasive element of your sales proposition.

Here is a checklist for you to test your sales math. How many of the following questions can you answer with confidence? You will find the answers at the end.

- What is EBIT and how is it calculated?
- What is APR and how is it calculated?
- What is ROI and how is it calculated?
- What is TCO and how is it calculated?
- What is TCA and how is it calculated?
- What is OPex and how is it calculated?
- What is the payback period for your solution and how is it calculated?
- What is Discounted Cash Flow and how is it calculated?
- What is Internal Rate of Return (IRR) and how is it calculated?
- What is the difference between direct and indirect costs?

- What is the difference between fixed and variable costs?
- What is the difference between mark-up and margin?
- What is Activity Based Costing?

Checking Your Score

How did you fare in the test? Count how many of the questions you could answer with confidence and check your score below:

11-13: Sales Math Genius – You are very confident when it comes to running the numbers and indeed could teach the customer a thing or two. Take care to slow down and engage – simply presenting the buyer with an ROI or cost benefit analysis is not enough. Indeed it may be counter-productive. If the buyer has not been involved in running the numbers he or she will struggle to either accept, or use them. Share your knowledge with the customer (as well as with others on your sales team).

8-10: Accomplished Sales Mathematician – You are engaging more with buyers around their numbers with the buyer and are starting to get to like math! It puts you ahead of your peers. However, there are times when you could still get caught out so deepening your knowledge is important. Keep on talking about numbers – even where the customer does not bring it up. Don't feel pressured to have all the answers – maybe the buyer does not have all the answers either. The objective is to work it out together. Focus on the questions that you struggled with, using the answers presented below as a starting point.

5-8: Budding Sales Mathematician – You are on a par, if not a little ahead of, your peers when comes to using numbers to sell. You are only rarely asked about the ROI and other aspects of the buyer's financial analysis. There are however signs that may be about to change. Why not sit down with a colleague in Procurement or Finance and learn a little more about how the benefits of your solution can be calculated. If you haven't got an ROI calculator or spreadsheet maybe it is time to build one. Maybe you need to be more proactive in engaging with buyers in 'running the numbers'. After all you don't want your competitors to be the first to take out the calculator.

1-5: Sales Math Beginner – You don't engage much with the buyer around his or her numbers. That could be a lost opportunity. Perhaps you are underestimating how important numbers are for what you are selling. So, why not ask your customers and prospects about the economics of their decision in order to understand whether it is important. When numbers are discussed you may be unconvincing. Given your knowledge of key terms / concepts, it is going to be difficult to quantify the benefits and to justify (from an economic point of view) the decision to buy your solution. A course in basic financial analysis may be required. Sit down with a colleague in Procurement or Finance and learn a little more about the importance of numbers in the buying decision. Ask for help in putting together a simple cost / benefits analysis for the customer.

Putting Your Sales Math to Work

Now that you have identified any information gaps in your sales math knowledge, don't stop there. Here is a more challenging test: how many of the above are you using in your selling:

Are terms such as ROI and TCO to be found in your sales presentations and sales proposals, as well as in your everyday conversations with customers and prospects?

Follow these steps to put numbers at the core of your selling:

- Focus on the questions that you struggled to answer. You will find **answers at the end**

- The test above included many of the most universal terms of importance in using numbers to sell. It is important to consider any specific financial terms and metrics used by your customers and their particular industry

- Get a calculator and use it in more of your sales meetings

- Read a financial statement for one of your customers!

- Sit with your accountant! The CFO in your company can help you develop the numbers aspect of your proposition, as well as your confidence in business or sales math generally

- Start to build a spreadsheet to calculate the impact of your solution, including TCO, ROI, etc

- Measure the impact of your products and solutions on your customer's business (and find out how they measure impact)

- Start talking to your prospects about their numbers from day one

- When you have sold to customers, keep the focus on 'the numbers' helping the buyer to track the results achieved and to measure progress against expectations.

The Answers to the Sales Math Quiz

The answers to the questions in the Sales Math Quiz are shown below.

Many of the terms used in finance at first can appear intimidating, however it is easier than you may think. To emphasize this point we have built the following answers using one of the most widely available sources there is, that is Wikipedia. They form a quick crash course in key financial terms that you are going to need in selling to today's numbers-obsessed buyers.

What is EBIT and how is it calculated?

In accounting and finance, earnings before interest and taxes (EBIT) is a measure of a firm's profit that excludes interest and income tax expenses. Operating income is the difference between operating revenues and operating expenses. When a firm has zero non-operating income, then operating income is sometimes used as a synonym for EBIT and operating profit.

What is APR and how is it calculated?

The term annual percentage rate (APR), also called nominal APR, and the term effective APR, also called EAR, describes the interest rate for a whole year (annualized), rather than just a monthly fee / rate, as applied on a loan, mortgage loan, credit card, etc. It is a finance charge expressed as an annual rate.

What is ROI and how is it calculated?

Return on investment (ROI) or rate of return (ROR), also known as 'rate of profit' or sometimes just 'return', is the ratio of money gained or lost (whether realized or unrealized) on an investment relative to the amount of money invested.

What is TCO and how is it calculated?

Total cost of ownership (TCO) is a financial estimate whose purpose is to help consumers and enterprise managers determine direct and indirect costs of a product or system. For example, the TCO defines the cost of owning an automobile from the time of purchase by the owner, through its operation and maintenance to the time it leaves the possession of the owner. Comparative TCO studies between various models help consumers choose a car to fit their needs and budget.

What is TCA and how is it calculated?

Total Cost of Acquisition (TCA) is a managerial accounting concept that includes all the costs associated with buying goods, services, or assets.

Generally, it is the net price plus other costs needed to purchase the item and get it to the point of use. These other costs can include the item's purchasing costs (closing, research, accounting, commissions, legal fees), transportation, preparation and installation costs.

Typically they do not include training or system integration costs that might be considered operational costs.

What is OPex and how is it calculated?

Operational expense, operational expenditure or OPex is an ongoing cost for running a product, business, or system.

In business, an operating expense is a day-to-day expense such as sales and administration, or research & development, as opposed to production, costs, and pricing. In short, this is the money the business spends in order to turn inventory into throughput.

What is the payback period and how is it calculated?

Payback period in capital budgeting refers to the period of time required for the return on an investment to 'repay' the sum of the original investment. For example, a $1,000 investment that returned $500 per year would have a two-year payback period. The time value of money is not taken into account. Payback period intuitively measures how long something takes to 'pay for itself'. All else being equal, shorter payback periods are preferable to longer payback periods.

What is Discounted Cash Flow / Internal Rate Of Return and how are they calculated?

Discounted Cash Flow is used to estimate the attractiveness of an investment opportunity. It uses future cash flow projections and discounts them to arrive at a present value. If the DCF of the IT project is higher than its anticipated current cost of the investment, the opportunity may be a good one based on the return generated – internal rate of return (IRR).

What is the difference between direct and indirect costs?

Indirect costs are costs that are not directly accountable to a cost object (such as a particular function or product). Indirect costs may be either fixed or variable. Indirect costs include administration, personnel and security costs, and are also known as overhead. These are costs that are not related to Production.

Direct costs are those for activities or services that benefit specific projects – for example, salaries for project staff and materials required for a particular project. Because these activities are easily traced to projects, their costs are usually charged to projects on an item-by-item basis.

What is the difference between fixed and variable costs?

Variable costs are expenses that change in proportion to the activity of a business. Variable cost is the sum of marginal costs over all units produced. It can also be considered normal costs. Fixed costs and variable costs make up the two components of total cost.

What is the difference between mark-up and margin?

Margin (on sales) is the difference between selling price and cost. This difference is typically expressed either as a percentage of selling price or on a per-unit basis. Managers need to know margins for almost all marketing decisions. Margins represent a key factor in pricing, return on marketing spending, earnings forecasts, and analyses of customer profitability.

What is Activity Based Costing?

Activity-based costing (ABC) is a costing model that identifies activities in an organization and assigns the cost of each activity with resources to all products and services according to the actual consumption by each. This model assigns more indirect costs (overhead) into direct costs compared to conventional costing models.

About the Authors

Ray and John are successful salespeople turned sales consultants. They come at selling from a new angle – that of the buyer. Focused on the high value, or complex, B2B sale, they have a unique insight into buying in large organizations. This is based on conversations with managers and buyers in some of the world's largest companies. That means they understand how sellers can turn the changes in the buying process, the business case and the buying team to their advantage.

Ray Collis has consulted to companies such as Smith+Nephew, Nilfisk, BT Wholesale and Norsk Hydro. He has Master's and Bachelor's degrees in Business and Marketing.

John O Gorman has sold and consulted internationally for organizations such as Digital, Compaq and Eontec (acquired by Siebel). He completed his International MBA in 2004 and holds a Bachelor of Commerce degree.

John and Ray act as sales advisors to ambitious sales organizations, government agencies and educational institutions. They are prolific writers on the subjects of buying and selling, as can be seen by the hundreds of articles, tips and techniques available at **www.sellerinsights.com** and **www.sellingintheclouds.com**.

The ASG Group
Accelerating Sales Growth

Ray and John established The ASG Group in 2007 as a specialist B2B sales consulting practice helping sales managers to boost sales. The letters ASG stand for Accelerated Sales Growth – the company's methodology for unlocking the hidden sales potential within sales organizations.

The company's ground-breaking research with many of the world's largest companies clearly pinpoints those strategies, skills and techniques most effective at winning the sale. The ASG Group uses this information to help managers to meet specific targets for win rates and sales growth.

The ASG Group's clients include some of the world's most successful sales organizations, including IBM, BT and Sage. The company's extensive library of best practice and, indeed, common practice in respect of sales and marketing enables managers to benchmark all aspects of sales team performance and potential.

The ASG Group
Accelerating Sales Growth
Unit 24 Parkwest Enterprise Centre,
Lavery Avenue, Dublin 12, Ireland.
www.theASGgroup.com

Lightning Source UK Ltd.
Milton Keynes UK
UKOW04f0221170914

238649UK00001B/45/P